The Jewish Struggle in the 21st Century

Personal/Public Scholarship

Series Editor

Patricia Leavy (*USA*)

Editorial Board

Carolyn Ellis (*University of South Florida, USA*)
Donna Y. Ford (*Vanderbilt University, USA*)
Henry Giroux (*McMaster University, Canada*)
Stacy Holman Jones (*Monash University, Australia*)
Sut Jhally (*University of Massachusetts, USA*)
Kip Jones (*Bournemouth University, UK*)
Jean Kilbourne (*Wellesley Centers for Women, USA*)
Peter McLaren (*Chapman University, USA*)

VOLUME 10

The titles published in this series are listed at *brill.com/pepu*

The Jewish Struggle in the 21st Century

Conflict, Positionality, and Multiculturalism

By

Daniel Ian Rubin

BRILL SENSE

LEIDEN | BOSTON

Cover illustration: Photograph by Daniel Ian Rubin

All chapters in this book have undergone peer review.

The Library of Congress Cataloging-in-Publication Data is available online at http://catalog.loc.gov

ISSN 2542-9671
ISBN 978-90-04-46406-3 (paperback)
ISBN 978-90-04-46407-0 (hardback)
ISBN 978-90-04-46408-7 (e-book)

Copyright 2021 by Daniel Ian Rubin. Published by Koninklijke Brill NV, Leiden, The Netherlands.
Koninklijke Brill NV incorporates the imprints Brill, Brill Hes & De Graaf, Brill Nijhoff, Brill Rodopi, Brill Sense, Hotei Publishing, mentis Verlag, Verlag Ferdinand Schöningh and Wilhelm Fink Verlag.
Koninklijke Brill NV reserves the right to protect this publication against unauthorized use. Requests for re-use and/or translations must be addressed to Koninklijke Brill NV via brill.com or copyright.com.

This book is printed on acid-free paper and produced in a sustainable manner.

ADVANCE PRAISE FOR
THE JEWISH STRUGGLE IN THE 21ST CENTURY

"Daniel Ian Rubin's *The Jewish Struggle in the 21st Century: Conflict, Positionality, and Multiculturalism* reflects on the increasing sense of marginality among American 'Jews' (however defined) as part of renewed focus on radical pedagogy in the schools and higher education. The social reality of 'Jews' in secular culture seems to have moved them from the historically defined 'perpetual victim' to positions of power, at least within a radical pedagogy that renders them 'White.' Rubin's first-rate study illuminates both the contentious function of 'race' as a fixed category as well as the question of the attribution of 'power' to groups that have been traditionally (and continue to be) marginalized. A solid and compelling study of the pitfalls of identity politics in American society, and specifically in higher education."
– **Sander L. Gilman, Distinguished Professor of the Liberal Arts and Sciences/Professor of Psychiatry, Emory University, author of *Jewish Self-Hatred***

"With inspiration from Warren Blumenfeld, I am moved by the author's activist intensity in addressing four questions: (1) What do you love about being your racial identity? (2) What has been difficult for you growing up this racial identity? (3) What do you never want to hear said again about or seen done to people of your racial identity group? and (4) How can people of other racial groups support you and be your allies? Daniel Rubin leads us all expertly in learning to create and navigate racially-inclusive cultures."
– **Virginia Stead, Founding Book Series Editor, Equity in Higher Education Theory, Policy, & Praxis**

*To my Jewish family –
the one that I have and the one I have lost*

CONTENTS

Foreword *Warren J. Blumenfeld*	xiii
Acknowledgments	xvii
Chapter 1: Introduction	1
Overview of Chapters	4
Chapter 2: Still Wandering: The Exclusion of Jews from Issues of Social Justice and Multicultural Thought	7
Background	7
Jews as a Minority Group	9
Jewish Exclusion in Multiculturalism	12
Teaching Antisemitic Awareness in Education	13
Conclusion	16
Implications	17
Chapter 3: Jews and Blacks in the Time of COVID-19: Solidarity and Conflict	19
Introduction	19
The Conflicted History of Black/Jewish Relations	20
Where Do We Go from Here?	24
Conclusion	26
Chapter 4: HebCrit: A New Dimension of Critical Race Theory	29
Introduction	29
HebCrit and Critical Race Theory	30
Jews Defined	32
Jews as a Persecuted Group	32
Jews and the Question of Race	34
Jews and the Tenuous "Space Between"	37
Jews and the Issue of Power	39
Critical Race Theory and Jewish Invisibility	40
HebCrit and Counternarratives	40
Conclusion	41

Chapter 5: Whiter Shade of Pale: Making the Case for Jewish Presence in the Multicultural Classroom — 43

Background — 43
Introduction — 43
Resurgent Antisemitism — 45
The Notion of "Whiteness" and White Identity — 46
Jewish Sense of Self — 49
Exclusion from Multicultural and Social Justice Discourse — 51
Conclusion — 53

Chapter 6: Navigating the "Space Between" the Black/White Binary: A Call for Jewish Multicultural Inclusion — 55

Introduction — 55
The Diversity and Multicultural Classroom — 56
Racialization and the Jews — 56
The Black/White Binary — 57
The "Space Between" — 59
The Negative Effects of Jewish Invisibility — 62
Conclusion — 63

Chapter 7: The Muddy Waters of Multicultural Acceptance: A Qualitative Case Study on Antisemitism and the Israeli/Palestinian Conflict — 65

Introduction — 65
Antisemitism and Multicultural Education — 66
Research Questions — 68
Methodology — 68
Theoretical Lens — 71
Zionism and the Israeli/Palestinian Conflict — 72
Results — 73
Discussion — 76
Conclusion — 78
Implications — 80

Chapter 8: Jewish Academics' Experiences of Antisemitism within the United States — 81

Introduction — 81
Perception of Antisemitism — 81

Hostility on U.S. Campuses	82
Methodology	83
Research Questions	84
Participant Information	84
Personal Experiences with Harassment	85
Professional Experiences of Harassment	88
Discussion	93
Conclusion	94
Future Research	95
Limitations	95

Chapter 9: The Stereotypical Portrayal of Jewish Masculinity on *The Big Bang Theory* — 97

Introduction	97
A Brief Depiction of the Jewish Male (and His Mother, of Course)	98
The Jewish Mother	100
The Television Depiction of the Jewish Male	101
The Wolowitz Conundrum	102
Representation of Judaism	104
Television, Stereotypes, and Perception	106
Conclusion	108
Implications	109

Chapter 10: Conclusion — 111

Reflection	112
Where Do We Go from Here?	113

References	115
About the Author	133

FOREWORD

As Wladylaw Szpilman, the protagonist in director Roman Polanski's film adaption of *The Pianist* (2002) remarks, "Sometimes I don't know which side of the wall I'm on." In *The Jewish Struggle in the 21st Century: Conflict, Positionality, and Multiculturalism*, Daniel Ian Rubin captures the tensions, the questions, the insecure and unsecured place of U.S. Jews – in particular, European-heritage Ashkenazim – in multiple sectors of life.

Rubin skillfully interweaves historical representations with current lived experiences of U.S. Jews, the bittersweet relationship between Jews and African Americans, and the gendered stereotypical depictions of Jewish males, while simultaneously confronting and expanding the continuum of this social notion we call "race." Throughout this examination, Rubin makes a compelling case for why the dearth of inclusion within the multicultural project regarding Jews and the oppressive condition of antisemitism must be confronted and changed, for this current exclusion seriously affects Jewish communities and scholars both within and outside academia. Depictions of Ashkenazim as "White" on the racial scale provide cover for multiculturalists in their justification to avoid discussions of antisemitism.

As Rubin addresses in this text, I have, myself, questioned my position along the racial spectrum. On numerous occasions, I have attended the annual National Gay and Lesbian Task Force's "Creating Change" conference, bringing together grass-roots activists from throughout North America as well as other countries around the world. At one of the conferences in the early 1990s, I was a participant in a well-attended workshop titled "Activists of Color/White Activists Dialogue" facilitated by two highly respected activists: a woman of color and a White Christian man.

When the workshop began, the woman outlined the agenda for the next one-and-one-half hours: the workshop would concentrate on the concepts of "race" and dialogue across racial divides, and it would include two separate panels of participant volunteers: one composed of four people of color, the other of four White people. Panel members were to each, in turn, answer four questions put to them by the facilitators, first the people of color panelists followed by the White people panelists.

The questions were: (1) "What do you love about being your racial identity?" (2) "What has been difficult for you growing up this racial identity?" (3) "What do you never want to hear said again about or seen done to people of your racial identity group?" and (4) "How can people of other racial groups support you and be your allies?"

As the facilitator explained the intended focus and agenda, great confusion came over me: Should I volunteer? Well, maybe, but I really can't because I'm not sure if either of the categories on which the panels are organized include me. I know for certain that I am not eligible to volunteer for the "persons of color" panel. But, also, I feel as if, somehow, I don't belong on the "White persons" panel either. Maybe I should just listen to the panelists, which I did.

But what caused my bewilderment? What got in my way of self-defining as "White"? From where was this feeling of not-belonging on either panel, or my feeling of in-betweenness coming? Thinking back, I came to realize that it stems, I believe, from both personal and collective experience.

For me, it seemed to have taken somewhat longer than, for example, many European-heritage Christians, to come to an acceptance that by dint of my skin color, hair texture, facial features, and most importantly, my European genealogy, U.S. society grants me a host of privileges denied those constructed as "persons of color." But then again, my father often talked about his childhood and the ways he suffered the effects of anti-Jewish prejudice. One of only a handful of Jews in his schools in Los Angeles in the 1920s and 1930s, many afternoons he returned home injured from a fight. During recess period in elementary school, to avoid attack by the other boys who targeted him as "the Jew," "the dirty Jew," and "the killer of Christ," he found an opening under one of the buildings where he hid each day. To get a decent job, his father, my grandfather Abraham, anglicized the family name, changing it from "Blumenfeld" to "Eddy Fields" so he could find a job within this highly discriminatory society.

When I was born in 1947, my maternal uncle's friend gave me a small gold chain with the fifth letter of the Hebrew alphabet, *Hei*, representing "G*d" in Hebrew, or "*HaShem*." Upon my Bar Mitzvah at the age of 13, my mother presented me with the *Hei*, saying: "Warren, you are old enough now to wear this. Remember, though, to always wear it *under* your shirt out of view. There are still many people who hate Jews, and I don't want you to get hurt if these people see the *Hei* around your neck."

Due to historical and social conditions, Jews have a sort of "double vision" (Brodkin, 1998) or "insider/outsider" status (Biale, Galchinsky, & Heschel, 1998) within contemporary U.S. society. Melanie Kaye/Kantrowitz concludes that:

> The truth is, Jews complicate things. *Jewish* is both a distinct category and an overlapping one...The problem is a polarization of white and color that excludes us. (1996, emphasis in original)

FOREWORD

Once constructed as the "Other" in European society, Jews and "Jewishness" in the U.S. – while certainly not fully embraced by the ruling elite as "one of their own" – becomes a sort of "middle" status, "standing somewhere between the dominant position of the White majority and the marginal position of people of color" (Biale, Galchinsky, & Heschel, 1998, p. 5). And this change in Jewish ethnoracial assignment has occurred only within the last 70 or so years.

Dominant groups have passed down stereotypes from generation to generation of Jews being the "killers of G*d," being in the service of the Devil, desecrators of the Christian Host, ritual murderers of Christian children, poisoners of drinking wells and transmitters of disease, being homeless wanderers, "clannish," cheating usurers, sexually perverse, being of an alien "race," being murderous Communists and Socialists who attempt to overthrow Capitalist systems, and simultaneously being enormously rich Capitalists, dominators of countries and world economies, and being exploiters of the oppressed.

It is no wonder that Jews as a community carry with them (us) an "oppression mentality," an "enemy memory" (Steele, quoted in Berman, 1994), or a "siege mentality" (Hertzberg, 1979), which is the intense awareness that anti-Jewish oppression can surface again at any time, regardless of how "good" conditions for Jews appear at any moment. With these lingering questions, with the occasional acts of anti-Jewish violence, with the continued categorization of Jews as "racially inferior" and as so-called "mud people" (along with people of color) by extremist White racist groups, and possibly because I continue to carry this "enemy memory," I come close to Brodkin's placement of Ashkenazi Jewish American ethnoracial assignment as "White," but not completely. I chose, therefore, to plot our current placement as "off-White" on the American ethnoracial scale as it is currently constructed.

In this text, Daniel Ian Rubin raises important issues related to Jewish heritage, identity, and "raciality," the place of Jews in discussions and education related to diversity, multiculturalism, and social justice, and how HebCrit fits within the overarching field of critical studies.

The Jewish Struggle in the 21st Century: Conflict, Positionality, and Multiculturalism will add significantly to the extant literature base on this deeply neglected field of inquiry.

Warren J. Blumenfeld
University of Massachusetts at Amherst

REFERENCES

Berman, P. (Ed.). (1994). *Blacks and Jews: Alliances and arguments*. Dell Publishers.
Biale, D., Galchinsky, M., & Heschel, S. (1998). *Insider/outsider: American Jews and multiculturalism*. University of California Press.
Brodkin, K. (1998). *How Jews became white folks & what that says about race in America*. Rutgers University Press.
Hertzberg, A. (1979). *Being Jewish in America*. Schocken Books.
Kaye/Kantrowitz, M. (1992). *The issue is power: Essays on women, Jews, violence, and resistance*. Aunt Lute Book.

ACKNOWLEDGMENTS

I want to thank Dr. Christine Sleeter and Dr. James Jupp for their thoughts and suggestions during my early research of Judaism, Whiteness, and multiculturalism.

I especially want to thank my colleague and friend of over a decade, Dr. Christopher Kazanjian. He has been my sounding board and unpaid editor since the beginning of this intellectual pursuit. His observations and insights have been invaluable to me.

CHAPTER 1

INTRODUCTION

As I sit to write the introduction to this book, I am once again reminded of the precarious position that Jews are situated in the United States. The night before the 2020 presidential election, a century-old Jewish cemetery in Grand Rapids, Michigan was vandalized, just hours before President Trump's last pre-election rally was to take place in that city. Several tombstones were spray-painted with red graffiti with messages of "TRUMP" and "MAGA" (Armus, 2020). Unfortunately, this is not an isolated incident for American Jews living in the twenty-first century.

> Nationally and statewide, reports of such attacks are also on the rise. More than 2,100 anti-Semitic incidents were reported to the ADL [Anti-Defamation League] in 2019, up 12 percent from the previous year and setting a record since the organization began tracking the data four decades ago. (Armus, 2020, para. 10)

With antisemitic events on the rise for several years in the U.S., it is no surprise that I have felt compelled to write this text. I am so thankful for the opportunity to share my thoughts with you, the reader.

The beginning of this text originated as just a thought in my mind while I was a doctoral student in Curriculum and Instruction in 2010. After first being introduced to the work of revolutionary critical pedagogist and scholar, Peter McLaren, I began to read all that I could about the theoretical framework of critical pedagogy. In brief, critical pedagogy is a mode of thought "preoccupied with social injustice and examines and promotes practices that have the potential to transform oppressive institutions or social relations, largely through educational practices" (Keesing-Styles, 2003, p. 3). While I was beginning to focus increasingly on issues of diversity and multiculturalism in both U.S. education and society, personal reflection and self-exploration were not even thoughts in my mind.

During the four and a half years of graduate school, I did not believe that my Jewish heritage and culture had much bearing on me or my study of others. The process of seeking understanding about issues of social justice, diversity, and critical/dialectical thought felt separate from my own life experiences. While I was taught to "unpack my invisible backpack" (McIntosh, 1989, p. 1) of the racial, cultural, religious, and socioeconomic privileges that made me who I was, there was no discussion of how being Jewish in U.S. society could have a negative impact on me as a person. My Jewishness[1] appeared to have little to no impact on my place in the modern multicultural world; to some extent, my Jewishness was simply deemed as unimportant. I was led to believe that Jewishness equaled Whiteness, and I did little to question that supposition. In my course offerings in multiculturalism and social justice, my Black, Latinx, Asian, Indigenous, Muslim, and Gay, Lesbian, Bisexual, Transgender, and Queer (GLBTQ) peers were addressed in-depth and with great alacrity, yet to my recollection, Jews were never mentioned in any assigned texts or group discussions. I felt uncomfortable during many class conversations because I had personal experience with microaggressions, hate speech, and being the Other as a Jewish person living in an area with few Jews. My experiences were never deemed important enough to discuss or engage. I felt alone and discounted. Something was just not right. Then, in an instant, everything changed.

One evening, during a class discussion in a doctoral-level social justice course, my perception of antisemitism (and my own self-understanding as a Jewish person) was turned on its head. As it will be discussed further in Chapter 2, a fellow graduate student made an antisemitic comment – unknowingly and without malice, I believe. This comment both shocked and infuriated me. That moment in time, and the feelings it aroused, had such a profound impact on me that it became the inspiration for a decade-long focus on antisemitism and Jewish positionality in multicultural education. I had realized that there was a major disconnect between the curricular content that I was studying at the university and my living relationship within it. I began to listen to my conscience when it told me that being Jewish in U.S. society was not the same as being White. There were obstacles and difficulties that did not appear to be understood by those unfamiliar with my Jewish background. Unfortunately, I had neither the ability to verbalize my feelings nor confidence to make any assertions about those thoughts at the onset of my research.

I learned quickly, upon embarking on my own personal study of a Jewish presence in issues of diversity and multiculturalism, that there really was very little information about Jews, antisemitism, or a Jewish place at the multicultural table. Collectively, Jews were either simply grouped in the

"White" category or mentioned in passing as an afterthought. This did not reflect how I thought about myself or my position in American society, and I felt obligated to affirm that Jews belong in the discussion of diversity and multiculturalism in both the university classroom and in the wider discussion of race.

In brief, this book details my journey, my intellectual development and new-found understanding, over the course of a decade. It began out of curiosity, focused on a search for self-understanding and a questioning of why there was so little Jewish presence in the university classroom. Over time, this shifted to a position of creation and confirmation of my desired place for a Jewish presence in U.S. society.

This decade of study culminated in a theory called HebCrit (pronounced "heeb" crit), which addresses Jewish people in Critical Race Theory (CRT) and is intended to pry open the door to the multicultural stronghold that Jews have long since been excluded. HebCrit can be defined as new critical theory that investigates issues of Jewish persecution in American society. The framework of HebCrit has five major assertions: (1) Jews continue to be discriminated against and persecuted; (2) Jews are a racialized group; (3) Jews, and their perception as White, creates invisibility and tension; (4) Jews' political and economic power is hyperbolic; and (5) Jewish personal stories have value.

There are several major foci that are woven throughout the text: Jewish multicultural inclusion, in both theory and practice; the complex Jewish positionality of light-skinned Jews in a country often seen as either Black or White; the notion of antisemitism and how Jewish people's lives are still affected, directly and/or indirectly, by anti-Jewish hatred, and Jews' relationship with people of color during the contentious age of Black Lives Matter and the COVID-19 pandemic.

The over-arching question that I will address in this text is as follows – what is the purpose of exploring the study of Jewish people, antisemitism, and the inclusion of the Jewish experience and their place in university multicultural discourse? As the coming chapters will demonstrate, there has certainly been resistance to my assertions about Jews "deserving" a place in multicultural thought, yet this book is not about the naysayers and excuse makers; it is about staking a claim that Jews are a discriminated minority group, both in the U.S. and around the globe, and they need to be explored and understood at a deeper level in order to address the complex positionality in which they are situated.

CHAPTER 1

OVERVIEW OF CHAPTERS

In Chapter 2, I discuss the idea that antisemitism, prejudice, and discrimination against Jewish people are still largely absent from the study of social justice issues and multicultural education at the university level in the U.S. Although often seen as being White, Jews are still discriminated against, with current reports showing that acts of antisemitism have been at their highest levels since World War II. There has also been a resurgence of antisemitic incidents at universities in the U.S., yet Jewish oppression is still neglected in multicultural/diversity classroom discussions. I will explain how this must change in order to create the next generation of social justice educators who can continue to deconstruct antisemitism.

Chapter 3 addresses the resurgence of antisemitic comments coming from Black celebrities, a brief overview of Black/Jewish relations, and how Jews and Blacks can further support each other as minority groups in the U.S. during these challenging times. While Blacks and Jews were seen as a relatively supportive force during the Civil Rights Movement, much of that solidarity has long since dissolved. During the time of the coronavirus and the protests for Black Lives Matter (BLM), many Jews continue to fight for the rights of the Black community, yet both groups continue to stumble over antiquated stereotypes and misunderstandings that impede their collective struggles.

In Chapter 4, I outline the foundational structure of a new critical theory called HebCrit that investigates issues affecting Jewish people in American society. HebCrit is rooted in Critical Race Theory, History, Social Psychology, Multicultural Education, and Jewish Studies. Jews continue to face specific concerns and obstacles in the both the United States and around the world (e.g., prejudice) and are often overlooked and ignored in multicultural, diversity, and ethnic studies. This section explains how this new theoretical framework provides a way to address the complicated positionality that many American Jews navigate on a daily basis.

In Chapter 5, I further explain how Jews living in the U.S. and the study of antisemitism continue to be overlooked in university multicultural and social justice classroom discussions. This is due to many factors, such as the misconceptions that Jews are solely a religious group, are White and have completely assimilated into American culture, and are economically successful. In order to validate the notion that Jews still face both racism and discrimination in the United States, I discuss why university multicultural and social justice programs must begin to discuss the issues pertaining to antisemitism.

In Chapter 6, I explore how diversity and multicultural analysis of race often falls along a Black/White binary paradigm. Therefore, those who are perceived to be White are often left out of the discussion of diversity and multicultural education (DME) in the United States. This absence is particularly true for American Jews of Ashkenazi descent. In academic circles today, the notion of Whiteness is often used as a determining factor for overlooking antisemitism while addressing issues of racism aimed at other racial and ethnic groups in the United States. I will explain how, due to a lack of acknowledgment in the university classroom, Jews continue to be overlooked in multicultural academic thought, which can have wide-ranging consequences for Jews and non-Jews alike.

Chapter 7 addresses Jews and antisemitism and how those scholars, determined to penetrate the walls of the multicultural education stronghold, are met with an ebb and flow of silence and vociferous resistance. A primary rationale for multiculturalists ignoring antisemitism appears to be the Zionist question and how they, themselves, perceive Israel's relationship with Palestine. I discuss my qualitative case study that analyzed interviews of six prominent scholars in the areas of multiculturalism, history, and Judaism through a critical pedagogical lens. In this chapter, I explore my personal experiences in regard to educational multiculturalists and the dismissal of Jews as a persecuted group. As a result, this chapter argues for the inclusion of the Jewish experience into university multicultural discourse.

Chapter 8 discusses the concept of antisemitism and how it can be perceived by American Jews who teach in the academe. Current data show that antisemitism on university campuses is on the rise in the United States, yet there are few studies that show how antisemitism affects the personal and professional lives of Jewish university professors. The presented mixed-method survey investigates Jewish university professors' (n = 93) experiences with antisemitism in both their past and present-day lives. The data show that the majority of study participants have had personal experiences with anti-Jewish harassment and discrimination at some point in their lives. In addition, a large number of the study participants have also faced antisemitism on their own university campuses. This study reinforces the notion that antisemitism continues to have negative consequences for Jewish members of U.S. society.

In Chapter 9, I delve into the negative stereotype of the weak, passive, Jewish male that has been a staple in the United States for well over a century. Even though there has been a larger Jewish presence on U.S. television over the past thirty years, the portrayal of Jewish men is still negative

CHAPTER 1

and stereotypical. On the popular syndicated comedy *The Big Bang Theory* [CBS, U.S.], the character of Howard Wolowitz is the quintessential emasculated, Jewish male stereotype. Through a lens of gender and masculinity studies, this chapter addresses the historical depiction of the Jewish male in U.S. society as well as popular television in the United States. How the consistent use of these negative stereotypes affects both Jews and non-Jews is also explored.

Chapter 10, the final chapter, explains the needs of the Jewish people in the twenty-first century and where we go from here as scholars belonging to a discriminated minority group. I also explain what I intend to study next as I continue my path of Jewish scholarship.

NOTE

[1] Defined as my religious, cultural, and linguistic sense of self.

CHAPTER 2

STILL WANDERING: THE EXCLUSION OF JEWS FROM ISSUES OF SOCIAL JUSTICE AND MULTICULTURAL THOUGHT

BACKGROUND

Growing up in a suburb in southern New York State, I was constantly reminded and reaffirmed of my Jewish identity. Everywhere I looked, I was greeted by Feinmans, Goldbergs, and Cohens. I drove by synagogues and Jewish delicatessens on a daily basis, and it wasn't uncommon to hear a smattering of Yiddish[1] along the way. I even had days off from school for Jewish high holidays (e.g., Rosh Hashanah) as well as the customary Christian holidays. But, despite the prevalence of Jews in my area, I was always aware of my Jewishness, my being different from the majority of Americans outside of my neighborhood. Whether it was being called "beagle beak" by a school custodian in fifth grade or hearing a customer in my favorite local pizza place yelling about how one of his customers "jewed" him out of a sum of money, I tangibly felt that of being the Other. Due to situations such as these, I was acutely aware that "words matter. They can cause damage. They have consequences" (Lasson, 2010, p. 451), This feeling has only increased as I have aged, matured, and moved far away from a Jewish hub like New York City.

After earning Bachelor's and Master's degrees in Arizona and Utah respectively, I moved to southern New Mexico and became a high school English teacher. There, I became even more aware of being on the outside of the dominant Christian culture. Langman (1995) asserted that, "Outwardly it may look as if Jews are perfectly at home in America, but this is misleading" (para. 10), which is definitely the case for many Jewish people just like me. I have become accustomed to playing the role of the token Jew (Altman et al., 2010) and the cultural outsider in a Christian country. For example, whenever my high-school students learned that I was Jewish through innocuous class conversation, you could often hear the collective shock and lilt in their voices as they said, in eerie unison, "You're Jewish?" like I just admitted to killing a man in cold blood and was now out on parole. This situation occurred almost every single year, without fail. Again, I was reminded of

© DANIEL IAN RUBIN, 2021 | DOI:10.1163/9789004464087_002

being different and felt like I was being looked upon with a gaze of both curiosity and astonishment.

When I became a doctoral candidate in the area of critical pedagogies in the Department of Education at New Mexico State University in Las Cruces, I began to learn about the struggle for social justice alongside my classmates, who consisted of African Americans, Asians, Mexicans/Mexican Americans, South and Central Americans, Haitians, Armenians, Dominicans, Indigenous Peoples, and members of the GLBTQ community, just to name a few. I remember quite clearly that I often glanced around my diverse, multicultural classrooms, and wondered where I fit in. I never really allowed myself to believe that I was a member of a discriminated minority group. My struggles with my Jewish identity, connections with mainstream culture, and underlying lack of acceptance (Altman et al., 2010) in an American society of Christian privilege (Schlosser et al., 2009) had flickered in and out of my mind throughout the duration of my studies in critical pedagogies and social justice. Because of the color of my skin, even as a Jew, I am simply seen as a White person (Langman, 1995). I mean, how could I possibly compare myself to a Black or Latinx person in modern society? The Holocaust was about 70 years ago; that's old news, right? We are a "model minority" (Freedman, 2005) now, so it's "all good." We live in a country that accepts us, and so on and so forth. Yet, I never truly believed any of that.

My journey to understanding Jewish positionality in the area of multiculturalism really began when I was in a whole-class discussion during a doctoral-level course called Social Justice Issues in Education. In this particular evening session, a classmate was recounting how she and her father (back in Haiti) haggled with the artists to try to buy their paintings for a cheaper price. Unfortunately, to my shock and dismay, she stated twice, without hesitation, that her uncle "Jewed"[2] the artists down in price. The comment came as such a surprise to me that I was literally speechless. I could not believe that a student, a doctoral student in critical pedagogy no less, could say such an ignorant and offensive thing. I was left staring at my hands in anger, with the professor only briefly mentioning that the student cannot say such things in his class, but there was absolutely no form of discussion or analysis about what just occurred. In addition, not one student in the class, several of them friends of mine, ever said a single word to me about the incident. It was soon after this event, and a great deal of personal reflection, that I realized that although my academic program covered important "issues of racism, sexism, classism, and heterosexism, little has been done in the area of anti-Semitism, the oppression of Jews" (MacDonald-Dennis, 2006, p. 267).

Current reports show that acts of antisemitism are at near-historic levels in the United States (ADL, 2019), and online/physical harassment and attacks on Jewish students are also at an all-time high in U.S. schools and universities (Anderson, 2020). Data show that:

> K-12 schools, as well as colleges and universities, continue to experience a significant number of antisemitic incidents. ADL recorded 411 incidents at K-12 non-Jewish schools in 2019 (up 19% from 344 in 2018), and 186 incidents at colleges and universities (down 10% from 201 in 2018). (Campus Safety, 2020, p. 2)

It is important to note that "religious-based hate crimes on college campuses roughly doubled between 2009 and 2017" (Gerstmann, 2020, p. 2). White Nationalist activity on college campuses from groups such as the Patriot Front, the American Identity Movement, and the New Jersey European Heritage Association has also increased drastically in recent years. For example, according to Bowden (2020), there was "a total of 630 instances of white nationalist propaganda distribution efforts across the reporting schools, an increase of 96 percent from 320 reported in 2018" (p. 1). Despite these concerning trends, Jewish oppression is still often neglected in diversity/multicultural education (DME) classroom discussions (Altman et al., 2010; MacDonald-Dennis, 2006; Rubin, 2018b, 2019). Even though antisemitism is a form of prejudice and discrimination (F. Cohen, 2010), it has been asserted that it "is likely that Jewish issues have been previously ignored because being Jewish is largely an invisible minority status" (Schlosser, 2006, p. 425), and in the eyes of some, they are even considered to be a "model minority" (Freedman, 2005).[3]

In this chapter, I will explain why Jews[4] are omitted from multicultural/social justice discussions in American university classrooms and why this must change in order to create the next generation of social justice educators who can continue to deconstruct antisemitism. I will also discuss how Jews see themselves, how they are perceived in American society, and what must be done to incorporate the topic of antisemitism into the discussions of multiculturalism and social justice issues.

JEWS AS A MINORITY GROUP

According to Schlosser (2006), "American Jews represent a small, yet culturally distinct community in the United States" (p. 434), and, based on the latest statistics, about 2.1% of the country's population is Jewish (Jewish

Population, 2020). By numbers alone, Jews are a very small minority group in the U.S. Unfortunately, the "fact that Jews are a minority is not widely acknowledged. Or, if they are acknowledged as a numerical minority, they are relegated to a status of somehow 'not counting' as a minority" (Langman, 1995, p. 2). Langman (1995) theorized that Jews are excluded from discussions of multiculturalism and social justice for four major reasons: (1) Jews are seen as being fully assimilated into American society; (2) they are viewed as being economically successful; (3) they are viewed as being members of the White majority; and (4) they are perceived to be members of a religious group and not a cultural group. Despite these false assumptions, Jews remain a discriminated group in the U.S. and face many of the same struggles as other minority groups of color.

Galchinsky (1994) stated that when "the word 'multicultural' is used, it is often used to mean 'people of color'" (p. 363), and since the majority of American Jews are seen as White (Altman et al., 2010), they are not allowed membership in the exclusive multicultural club. It is important to note that although most American Jews are seen as White, and therefore, are able to benefit from their White privilege (Langman, 1995), that in no way means that Jews are free from persecution and discrimination; that is far from the truth. Schlosser (2006) has asserted that "[m]any American Jews will have a personal experience with anti-Semitism at some point in their lives…[and] nearly all Jews are impacted by acts of anti-Semitism vicariously" (p. 433); therefore, they continue to be discriminated against by members of American society. Lea and Sims (2008) explained that, "Whiteness is a complex, hegemonic, and dynamic set of mainstream socio-economic processes, and ways of thinking, feeling, believing, and acting (cultural scripts) that function to obscure the power, privilege, and practices of the dominant social elite" (pp. 1–2), and since Jews are viewed as White in American society, logic dictates that Jews are now considered oppressors as well (along with their White brethren). Therefore, it may be believed that Jews are not part of the multicultural discussion in the U.S. due to their new role as oppressors of people of color. McLaren (1995) posited that, "Whites will often think of their Scottishness, Irishness, or Jewishness, and so on, before they think of their whiteness" (p. 52). Contrary to McLaren's assertion, Jews have an incredibly long history of being oppressed and victimized by Whites, yet somehow, they are now put into the same category as those who have been their tormenters (Langman, 1995).

Studies have shown that Jews think of themselves as both Jews and Americans (Schlosser et al., 2009), and they often feel conflicted over how to maintain their Jewish identity (Altman et al., 2010). I would speculate that most Jews do not think of themselves as being Jewish first to avoid the discussion of Whiteness, but rather often refer to themselves as Jews first because their "very existence is perennially in question" (Langman, 1995, p. 3). It is a question of preservation, not maintaining and/or justifying an elite status in this country, which helps determine a Jewish person's sense of identity (Schlosser, 2006).

Alba (2006) observed that, "American Jews…have had a major impact on relatively elite strata of their society's culture. The impact is apparent if one looks at the intellectual, artistic, and scientific aspects of the mainstream culture" (p. 351), yet this does not mean that Jews are a fully accepted part of American society. Following that line of logic, it is like saying that just because the U.S. has had a Black president, Black people are completely equal members of our racially stratified and hegemonic society. Similarly, just because many people love the music of Neil Diamond, reruns of *Seinfeld*, and watching Gal Godot and Adam Sandler films does not, in any way, mean actual societal acceptance of Jewish people. It is situational and hollow, an acceptance based on tolerance in small doses and in confined, pre-determined spaces. It is because of this basic fact that I believe firmly that Jews should be given the opportunity to be discussed and studied as a discriminated and subjugated group in a university class setting, just the same as people of color.

There are those in the U.S. (and around the world) who still believe negative misconceptions and stereotypes about Jewish people, such as, they have a "propensity for financial chicanery and bad bargains…or even worse, the lingering sense that they were Christ-killers in league with the Devil" (Freedman, 2005, p. 75). Due to these false and harmful beliefs, Jews have been victims of antisemitism for over 4000 years. Antisemitism is exhibited in several forms, such as the use of stereotypes, various forms of oppression and discrimination, segregation, and ultimately, genocide (Schlosser, 2006). According to the most recent FBI hate crime statistics, antisemitism is not only alive and well in the U.S., but also growing. The hate crime data show that, "Of hate crime offenses motivated by religious bias in 2019, 60.3% were anti-Jewish" (Donaghue, 2020, para. 9). Jewish people, by far, have the largest percentage of victims on the anti-religion hate crime list. For the sake of comparison, the next closest group was an anti-Islamist bias, at 13.2% (FBI, 2020, para. 6). It is also important to note that in 2019, anti-Jewish hate crimes increased by 14% (Donaghue, 2020, para. 10). This type of data

CHAPTER 2

is difficult to swallow in the twenty-first century. Galchinsky (1994) encapsulated the concerns of the modern Jew in the United States when he stated that:

> We have watched the incidence of anti-Semitism increase and spread in the new nations of Eastern Europe, in the unified Germany, in France, in Britain, and in our own backyards. When Plymouth Rock has a swastika on it, and my grandfather's tombstone is overturned by the KKK, and the Jewish Federation at which I used to work receives bomb threats, and the local Jewish bookstore receives White Aryan Resistance literature, and my friend's synagogue has been set on fire, I begin to feel endangered. (p. 367)

Jews are still discriminated against in the U.S. and are victim to the highest percentage of reported anti-religion hate crime, yet they are not covered in most university discussions of multiculturalism and social justice in the United States. This needs to change.

JEWISH EXCLUSION IN MULTICULTURALISM

From my own studies of multiculturalism through various classes in my doctoral program, there had never once been a discussion of Judaism or antisemitism. Through various texts (e.g., *Deculturalization and the Struggle for Equality: A Brief History of the Education of Dominated Cultures in the United States* by Spring, 2010), we covered discrimination against women, Blacks, Native Americans, Asian Americans, Latinxs, and members of the GLBTQ community, yet, as Kremer (2001) stated in regard to their discussion in a multicultural context, the study of Jews is practically nonexistent. She asserted:

> Multicultural literature, as currently identified in anthologies and college courses is not, as the name suggests, open to varied cultures. Instead, it is a restricted venue clearly posting 'not wanted' signs for ethnic Euro-American literatures and Jewish American literature. If the literature is not African-, Asian-, Hispanic- or Native-American or another literature designated as produced by 'people of color,' that has been marginalized, it is excluded or excised from the anthologies, and therefore absent from the multicultural classroom. (p. 318)

Although there appears to be no widespread study investigating the absence of Judaism in multicultural anthologies, of the major edited texts discussing multiculturalism and/or social justice that I covered in university courses (e.g., *Critical Pedagogy and Race* by Leonardo, 2005; *Multicultural Education, Critical Pedagogy, and the Politics of Difference* by Sleeter & McLaren, 1995; *Teaching for Social Justice* by Ayers et al., 1998) there is no discussion of Jews as being a discriminated minority group and little mention of Jews at all. It has been asserted by Furman (2000) that Jews are not considered a part of American multiculturalism, partially because they are perceived as having "made it" in American society and are no longer struggling nor suffering economically and/or politically in the U.S.

In the area of multicultural literature, Furman (2000) and Rubin (2004) noted the gross absence of Jewish American writers in anthologies devoted to minority and multicultural literature (e.g., in the *Heath Anthology of American Literature*, 1998), and I have noticed the same in my own personal research and readings, where there is no mention of Jews as being a subjugated minority group (e.g., as in *Critical Multicultural Analysis of Children's Literature* by Botelho & Rudman, 2009; *Handbook of Research on Children's and Young Adult Literature* by Wolf et al., 2011). Following suit, in the area of children's picture books, according to Cummins (2001), "The fact is that Jews have not been invited to the multicultural party. Many anthologies promoting multicultural literature divide themselves into sections based on different races and ethnicities, and Jews are often left out" (p. 3). No matter the perception of Jewish Americans or the rationale for their exclusion from multicultural literature, as was previously discussed, there has been a resurgence of antisemitism in both the U.S. and around the world. In order to help combat antisemitism, Jews must begin to be addressed in multicultural discussions in the university classroom.

TEACHING ANTISEMITIC AWARENESS IN EDUCATION

Like MacDonald-Dennis (2006), I believe that "studying Jewish oppression and anti-Semitism should be more fully incorporated into social justice and anti-racist education programs" (p. 275). It is essential that antisemitism be discussed at the university level alongside prejudice, discrimination, and the history of violence against all peoples of color and sexual orientation. There are no acceptable reasons why Jewish Americans are not a part of this critical discourse.

I believe that the question that needs to be asked of my fellow educators is, "How can those working in the areas of social justice and multiculturalism help deconstruct biases and misconceptions while educating people

CHAPTER 2

about antisemitism?" Primarily, it is essential that "teacher education…be reformed so that teachers can examine their own personal knowledge and values" (Banks, 2005, p. 106). Future educators need the time and support to be able to dig deep within themselves and uncover all of their subjectivities and hidden biases; it is only after this process that they can then assist their students to reflect upon their own subjectivities and racial/ethnic assumptions of Jewish people. This reflective process can be accomplished at all levels of study – undergraduate to doctoral level. There are many ways to accomplish this task: through critical self-reflection (Hackman, 2005; Rios et al., 2003), reflexive analysis and deconstruction of one's own personal/historical contexts (Haynes Writer & Chávez Chávez, 2001), personal inventories of one's own social identities (Harro, 2000), community analysis projects (Haynes Writer & Baptiste, 2009), critical discussions about diversity and social justice issues (Hackman, 2005), and perspective-taking exercises as the "Other" (Rios et al., 2003). According to Cochran-Smith et al. (2010):

> Teacher education for social justice encompasses many pupil learning goals, including thinking critically, connecting knowledge to real-world problems and situations, challenging received knowledge, understanding multiple perspectives, debating diverse viewpoints, unpacking underlying assumptions, and engaging productively in cross-cultural discussion. (p. 37)

In other words, there are many effective teaching techniques and learning strategies to help students become aware of their own "blind spots" in their own personal understanding. King (1991) echoed this sentiment when she stated that "students need experiential opportunities to recognize and evaluate the ideological influences that shape their thinking about schooling, society, themselves, and diverse others" (p. 143). In order to do this, students must be exposed to all oppressed racial/ethnic groups in this country, not just non-Jewish people of color. When Jews are absent from the discussion of social justice issues, they are denied the opportunity for compassion and genuine understanding.

Although research has shown that "psychologically, individuals resist having to consider information that challenges their own thinking and, most especially their self-image" (Rios et al., 2003, p. 12), students must be pushed to a level of discomfort in order for them to come to terms with their own true beliefs about Jewish people. Change does not often come without some form of discomfort. There can be no shift in one's thinking if there is no discussion and/or (re)education. According to Ladson-Billings

(1996), "Beginning to speak about race can open up avenues of possibility for speaking about other forms of marginalization and oppression" (p. 251). Therefore, engaging in critical thought can lead to other pathways of personal discovery as well as leading to a better understanding of all people of color and racial/ethnic diversity.

For classroom teachers and university professors, I highly recommend expanding outside of the popular and commonly used multicultural anthologies to approach antisemitism. There are a plethora of journal articles that address discrimination against Jews (e.g., "Including Jews in Multiculturalism" by Langman, 1995), yet it will take some effort from the instructor to find them; therefore, I suggest using my references as a starting point. In particular, I highly recommend reading *Contemporary Jewish American Writers and the Multicultural Dilemma: Return of the Exiled* by Furman (2000) and *Jewish Issues in Multiculturalism: A Handbook for Educators and Clinicians* by Langman (1999). They both do a very good job of summarizing discrimination of Jewish Americans as well as explaining issues regarding Jewish Americans' place in multicultural literature. I would also suggest visiting the website of the Anti-Defamation League (www.adl.org) in order to learn about the various issues affecting the Jewish community, both in the United States and around the globe.

In regard to classroom practice, there are several units/activities that I use to introduce students to antisemitism and discrimination. In particular, with my junior-level high school English/Language Arts classes, I read a novel titled *My Name is Asher Lev*. Written by Chaim Potok (2003), *My Name is Asher Lev* is about a young boy growing up in a deeply conservative Hasidic community who struggles to find a balance between his art and his faith. Through the teaching of this engaging novel, I introduced antisemitism in the United States. I printed and distributed recent hate group maps from the Southern Poverty Law Center (SPLC), and together we discussed the various groups, some in our own backyard, that had a deep hatred for Jews. I also created a handout composed of various antisemitic cartoons from the hate group called the White Aryan Resistance (www.resist.com), and as a class, we explored hatred in its most virulent forms. In my Latinx Literature class, while covering our unit on personal identity, I introduced the notion of the "crypto-Jew" (Crenson, 2006). In brief, after the beginning of the Spanish Inquisition, many Jews were expelled from the Iberian Peninsula; therefore, many Latinxs have lived for centuries completely unaware of their hidden Jewish pasts.

CHAPTER 2

In the classroom, I would also suggest discussing issues pertaining to Jews in addition to the Holocaust and popular religious holidays, such as Hanukkah. Talking about the Holocaust has great value in the classroom, and the reality is that, "Americans know far too little about the Holocaust and the consequences are touching communities across the country" (Barall & Paolozzi, 2020, p. 1). Yet, other examples of antisemitism are often overlooked in public education and need to be addressed. Similarly, even though it is important to recognize non-Christian holidays, the discussion of Jewish holidays has minimal importance when compared to issues of discrimination and persecution.

CONCLUSION

Although it is assumed that Jews in the U.S. are members of the White majority, are successful economically, and have achieved success in the public eye (e.g., that of movie stars), that does not tell the whole story of Jews in America. Many Jews live in poverty. Many Jews are victims of abuse and discrimination. Many Jews are accepted in American society until they are discovered to be Jews, so they live with their Jewishness hidden beneath the surface for fear of what will come (Altman et al., 2010). Therefore, just because many Jews are light skinned does not mean that they are accepted fully into American society.

According to MacDonald-Dennis (2006), "Because non-Jews do not include Jewish issues in multiculturalism, I argue that this tells that their experience is of no importance and exacerbates Jewish students' invalidation of Jewish identity and anti-Semitism" (p. 276). Due to the discrimination, prejudice, and oppression of the Jewish people in the United States, they should be discussed alongside their brothers and sisters of color. Jews should not be ignored again and sent packing across the land looking for acceptance, like the proverbial wandering Jew. Throughout the history of the Jewish people, the notion of fighting for social justice has been a deeply ingrained principle (Schlosser, 2006). Jews have been fighting for social justice of peoples of color throughout modern history (e.g., during the Civil Rights movement) (Baker et al., 2007), and they have walked side by side, hand in hand, with those who deserved recognition, fairness, and equality. Yet, due to a variety of reasons that will be discussed in the coming chapters, Jews are not yet members of the multicultural club in the U.S. In the areas of social justice and multiculturalism, Jews are simply ignored. It is for these reasons that I feel that, "Jews must be included under the multicultural umbrella because however few in number and whether by choice or assignment by others, we remain a distinct ethnic and religious group in American life" (Cummins, 2001, p. 6).

Now is the time for educators, theorists, and multiculturalists to bring antisemitism into the fold and teach it at the university level, especially for those who intend to be future educators. According to Giroux (1997):

> In order for teachers, students and others to come to terms with 'whiteness' existentially and intellectually, we need to take up the challenge in our classrooms and across a wide variety of public sites of confronting racism in all its complexity and ideological and material formations. (p. 385)

It is the responsibility of all multicultural educators to help break down the negative falsehoods perpetrated against Jewish people in order to welcome them into the circle of social justice, once and for all.

IMPLICATIONS

It is important to note that the fight against antisemitism is not just the responsibility of the Jews, but rather, all Americans (Lasson, 2010), since, "Today's antisemitism becomes tomorrow's anti-someone else" (Lightman, 2010, p. 375). University professors, along with the textbook authors and manufacturers who supply texts to the professors, are obligated to include Jews in their anthologies about social justice issues and multiculturalism. The fight against injustice extends across all color lines and sexual orientations, and this war must begin to be waged in the university classroom. Ultimately, there are some Jews who believe that "the world is witnessing a new, virulent, globalizing, and even lethal anti-Jewishness reminiscent of the atmosphere of Europe in the 1930s" (MacDonald-Dennis, 2006, p. 272), and, with this being the case for many American Jews, the time to properly educate its citizens is now.

ACKNOWLEDGMENT

An earlier version of this chapter appeared as: Rubin, D. I. (2013). Still wandering: The exclusion of Jews from issues of social justice and multicultural thought. *Multicultural Perspectives*, *15*(4), 213–219 (https://doi.org/10.1080/15210960.2013.844607). Used here and modified with permission from the publishers.

CHAPTER 2

NOTES

1. Defined as "the language of the Ashkenazic Jews of Central and Eastern Europe…[where] Germanic grammar and vocabulary is mixed with Hebrew and Aramaic, and sprinkled with words from Slavic and ancient Romance languages" (Johnson, 1996, p. 1).
2. An offensive way to describe the process of haggling down prices, often unfairly and unscrupulously.
3. A model minority is seen by society as being economically successful, high achieving (academically), and one that causes few problems for the mainstream culture (Freedman, 2005; Yu, 2006).
4. Referring to White Jews in the United States. While there are certainly Jews of color living in the U.S., such as African, Latinx, and Asian Jews (Rishon, 2015), the focus on this chapter is on those perceived as being White.

CHAPTER 3

JEWS AND BLACKS IN THE TIME OF COVID-19: SOLIDARITY AND CONFLICT

INTRODUCTION

I mentioned previously that the fight against antisemitism cannot be fought by Jews alone. The Jewish people need support from people of color in order to eliminate antisemitism once and for all (if that is even possible). While completing the writing of this book, the United States is in a state of great tumult. First came COVID-19 in February 2020, the first major viral pandemic in a century, which has led to more than 540,000 American deaths (as of press time). Then came the murder of George Floyd at the hands of Minneapolis police, which some were calling the tipping point of race relations that "captured the public consciousness unlike few other events in American history" (Nakhaie & Nakhaie, 2020, p. 1). While focusing on writing this text, attempting to keep me and my family safe from the coronavirus, and protesting for the Black Lives Matter (BLM) movement, which calls for an end to police brutality, racial inequality, and systemic racism in the U.S., I was taken aback by an apparent reemergence of antisemitism from several Black sports and entertainment celebrities. It all began when National Football League (NFL) star wide receiver DeSean Jackson of the Philadelphia Eagles:

> posted two images on his Instagram story quoting Hitler as saying white Jews 'will blackmail America. [They] will extort America, their plan for world domination won't work if the Negroes know who they are. The white citizens of America will be terrified to know that all this time they've been mistreating and discriminating and lynching the Children of Israel. (Seifert, 2020, pp. 2–3)

Not only is the quote misattributed to Adolph Hitler, but it is also grossly and egregiously antisemitic, whether the message was intended that way or not.

Then came similar antisemitic comments from rapper Ice Cube, former National Basketball Association (NBA) player Stephen Jackson, and television host Nick Cannon, all espousing the words of Nation of Islam leader

CHAPTER 3

Louis Farrakhan. Minster Farrakhan has demonized and scapegoated Jews for decades and continues to spread conspiracy theories that Jews control banks, Hollywood and the media, the FBI, and even world governments, such as that of Mexico (Cohen, 2020; Kirchick, 2018). The string of antisemitic statements and posts were coming out so fast and furious that the Black-Jewish Alliance of the Antidefamation League (2020) was compelled to make a statement condemning antisemitism and the need for a continued partnership between the Black and Jewish communities in order to fight against hatred. Even former NBA great Kareem Abdul-Jabbar (2020) felt the need to write an editorial for the *Hollywood Reporter* denouncing the reemergence of Jewish stereotypes and racism. Then came the most heinous comments from British rapper Wiley on Facebook and Twitter, when he called Jews "snakes" and "cowards" and insinuated that Jewish people are comparable to the racist Ku Klux Klan (Beaumont-Thomas, 2020; Kirka, 2020).

Hill (2020) noted that "the unfortunate truth is that some Black Americans have shown a certain cultural blind spot about Jews. Stereotypical and hurtful tropes about Jews are widely accepted in the African American community" (p. 3). Unfortunately, current data supports that notion. According to Kirchick (2018), "Attitudinal surveys conducted by the ADL consistently show that African Americans harbor 'anti-Semitic proclivities' at a rate significantly higher than the general population (23 percent and 14 percent respectively in 2016)" (p. 5). Despite having a shared history of overcoming and surviving oppression, as well as fighting together during the Civil Rights movement, it now appears that Jewish and Black people find themselves set against one another (Schlosser et al., 2007). Many Jewish organizations vehemently support the BLM movement (e.g., the Union for Reform Judaism, T'ruah, Jews for Racial and Economic Justice), and it is my hope that there can be a significant change in Jewish/Black relations coinciding with the improved treatment of Black people in the U.S.

THE CONFLICTED HISTORY OF BLACK/JEWISH RELATIONS

History has shown that the fates of Blacks and Jews were intertwined (Shapiro, 1994). Both communities have had a fairly strong and mutually advantageous relationship, but the relationship, like all relationships, has been filled with tension and conflict (Morris & Rubin, 1993). It has been asserted that soon after their initial arrival in the U.S., "Jews played an important role in advancing the civil rights of, and furthering opportunities for, African Americans, whose fate Jews considered intertwined with their own as fellow minorities in a WASP-dominated country" (Kirchick, 2018, pp. 8–9). It was not lost on many Jews that their vast experience with oppression and antisemitism parallels centuries of Black racism, discrimination, and oppression (Schlosser et al., 2007).

The reality is that for most of the United States' history, the Jewish and Black communities were separated by both geography and demographics. Until the twentieth century, Jews predominantly lived north of the Mason-Dixon line, while the majority of Blacks lived in the south (Greenberg, 2010). The issue of slavery, the racial elephant in the room, has long been a contentious topic between Blacks and Jews. There have been allegations from the Historical Research Department of the Nation of Islam in *The Secret Relationship between Blacks and Jews*, that Jews financed and dominated in the African slave trade (Faber, 1998). Let me first say that it was both disheartening and upsetting for me to learn during my research for this text that southern Jews did engage in the slave trade, and it has been reported that 25% of southern Jews owned slaves (Greenberg, 2010). Yet, while that percentage appears quite high, it is important to remember that Jewish participation in slavery was miniscule, especially in comparison to their non-Jewish peers (Drescher, 1993; Faber, 1998; Korn, 1961). The idea that the Jews dominated the U.S. slave trade is simply unfounded and untrue. The fact of the matter was that there were very few Jewish planters in the Old South; Southern Jews had neither the wealth nor the status to own large plantations. In the nineteenth century, Jewish immigrants were much more likely to be storekeepers or peddlers than farmers (Korn, 1961). Just like other new immigrants to the U.S., Jews embraced the attitudes and opinions of their new surroundings because they wanted to fit in and be successful in their new homeland (Korn, 1961). Perry and White (1986) contended that:

> The acceptance of the racial status quo by Jews in the South was not only practical in term of the risks associated with opposing slavery and the economic benefits associated with participating in the slave business; it was also self-serving in the sense that the presence of slaves prevented Jews from being at the bottom of the social system and thus insulated them from the dis-advantages attendant to such social position. (pp. 51–52)

In addition, Greenberg (2010) affirmed that, "Southern Jews feared that challenging racial hierarchies so central to southern white identity would fan the flames of anti-Semitism" (p. 15). Being seen as White meant relative safety for the Jewish people, and they did little to bring attention to themselves

CHAPTER 3

out of self-preservation. The reality is that whether it be for humanitarian or self-serving reasons, Jews often maintained the White status quo in the south for their own safety and social status. That being said, Korn (1961) noted that many Jews "were appalled at human exploitation of the life and labor of other human beings. Most of them reacted in a purely personal way, by avoiding the owning of slaves or by helping slaves" (p. 196). Therefore, few Jews actually owned slaves, either due to personal or financial reasons, and many were disgusted by the notion of slavery.

Race relations between Jews and Blacks continued to grow after the Civil War came to an end. As mentioned previously, few Jews actually lived in the southern U.S. during the mid-nineteenth century, yet after the Civil War, those Jews who were working in the south were much more willing to serve Black people than White businesses (Greenberg, 2010). Foner (1975) explained that during the nineteenth century, "Jews alone among whites in America, whether native-born or immigrants, were viewed as sharing with black people the status of second-class citizenship" (p. 360). This second-class status appeared to have begun to forge a bond between the Black and Jewish communities.

By the turn of the twentieth century, hundreds of thousands of rural southern Blacks began to move to large cities in the North hoping for better lives (Greenberg, 2010). According to Perry and White (1996), "[An important] development in black-Jewish relations in the first half of the twentieth century involved the emergence of a cooperative relationship in the pursuit of increased rights and opportunities for blacks" (p. 54). Jews became supporters of the Black community early on, and they worked alongside each other for the common goal of improved quality of life whenever possible (Morris & Rubin, 1993). This is evident due to the fact that Jews played a prominent role in the establishment of the National Association for the Advancement of Colored People (NAACP) in 1910 (Perry & White, 1996; Webb, 1998). During the twentieth century, "Both communities recognized reasons to cooperate, but also found themselves at odds given the asymmetries between them in class, historical experience, and racial identity" (Greenberg, 2010, p. 16). In the early/mid twentieth century, Jews simply had better economic and social opportunities than Blacks did because they were frequently considered to be White; Jews were often spared the racism and oppression that the Black community was subjected to (Schlosser et al., 2007).

It was also during this time that the Black community became increasingly concerned with Jews and what was perceived as questionable business practices and dominance over economic sectors in the U.S. (Perry & White,

1996; Sigelman, 1995). In particular, the relationships of landlord/tenant and merchant/customer in the inner cities played out negatively for race relations between the two groups (Perry & White, 1996). The relationship between Blacks and Jews did improve after Adolph Hitler and the Third Reich came to power in Germany. Due to the horrible treatment of the Jewish people, and the eventual extermination of Jews in the Holocaust, Blacks became supportive and sympathetic of the Jews by the end of WWII (Perry & White, 1996). This change in relationship "was attributable to their realization that they shared a history of discriminatory treatment and that at this time in history, conflict between them was not to the advantage of either" (Perry & White, 1996, p. 56).

It is well-documented that Jews played an important role in the Civil Rights Movement (Dollinger, 2018; Webb, 1998). This period of time may be considered by some to be the pinnacle of Jewish/Black cooperation and support (Morris & Rubin, 1993). Morris and Rubin (1993) explained that Blacks and Jews:

> became strong, resourceful allies in the long, costly struggle for civil rights in the courts and in the streets. Throughout, the Jewish community consistently stood out to blacks as the most supportive white population group by far. Through these activities, black and Jewish leaders gradually forged strong, close ties that probably reached their peak in the major legislative triumphs of the mid-1960s. (p. 44)

Jewish organizations helped push for the passage of the 1964 Civil Rights Act and supported the work of the NAACP and other prominent groups at the time (Perry & White, 1996). According to Greenberg (2010):

> Jews, for reasons of both self-interest and their understanding of their ethnic and religious heritage, embraced the cause of civil rights more energetically than any other white group. Many communities experienced persecution; only Jews chose to devote a large proportion of their own agencies' agendas to issues of African American equality. And Jews made up a disproportionate number of the white contributors to and activists in the civil rights movement. If their commitment was less avid than many now like to claim, certainly it was greater than that of other white communities. (p. 252)

During the 1950s and first half of the 1960s, Jews gave substantial legal, financial, and organizational resources to the Civil Rights Movement, but of course, not everything is as it seems. During this time, Jews were beginning

CHAPTER 3

to be seen as middle-class Whites and were moving out to White suburbs, which were still prohibited to Blacks by exclusive bylaws. Many Jews still owned businesses in the inner cities, and there, Jews were accused of price gouging, running second-rate apartment buildings, and taking capital out of Black neighborhoods (Dollinger, 2018). Jewish support for civil rights began to wane in the mid-1960s due to the rise of the Black Power movement (Perry & White, 1996). There were sporadic flare-ups between Black and Jewish communities after the Civil Rights movement ended, such as the New York City school strike of 1968 and the Crown Heights (NY) riot of 1991 (Kramer, 1985; Wax-Thibodeaux, 2020).

As is evident, the history of the Blacks and the Jews in the U.S. is a complicated topic. While seemingly quite positive at times, their relationship has had its high and low points; unfortunately, historians cannot seem to come to a consensus, even when discussing the same exact time period. Some seem to glorify the relationship between the groups as being stellar, especially during the Civil Rights era, but there are many reports that conflict that rosy image. Despite what has occurred in the past (or because of it), Katz and Lipstadt (2020) asserted correctly that, "Like so many white Americans, Jews need to ask hard questions about their white racial privilege, their part in a system of racial injustice, and explore how they can better engage in the work of rooting out racism from our society" (p. 4).

WHERE DO WE GO FROM HERE?

Unfortunately, many people in the U.S. feel that Black/Jewish relations have been declining over time (Morris & Rubin, 1993), and this is where we find ourselves today – confronting an antisemitic assault by Black celebrities and athletes. Blake (2020) believed adamantly that:

> These stories about supposed Black-Jewish tensions fit a pattern. They hibernate and then re-emerge every couple of years to feed a perception that there is pervasive anti-Semitism in the Black community or some historical 'tension' between Black people and Jews. But that perception is bogus. No one should let the uninformed musings of a few Black celebrities convince us otherwise. Talk to many people who know the history of both groups and they will tell you the same. (p. 2)

While I appreciate Blake's vigorous optimism, recent research has shown trends that are more concerning. It has been found that, "More than a quarter of African Americans (28%) say they are seeing more black people they know express anti-Semitism than in the past...[and about] 1 in 5 (19%) believe Jewish people are blocking black progress in the United States" (Earls, 2019, p. 4). In other words, it is truly hard to know who to believe in racial matters such as these. It does seem that most Black people do not seek conflict with Jews and vice versa (Kirchick, 2018), yet the tension between the two groups persist.

It has been stressed that Jews and Blacks share many common beliefs, cultural values, traditions, and policy interests (Morris & Rubin, 1993; Schlosser et al., 2007). In particular, both groups have a dangerous common enemy – White supremacy (Belding-Zidon, 2020). Katz and Lipstadt (2020) noted that, "Indeed, anti-Jewish and anti-Black hatreds are not only parallel but often interconnected. Though it is too often ignored, both anti-Semitism and anti-Black racism lie at the core of White supremacist ideology" (p. 3). While it is true that White supremacy is a more pressing threat to Blacks at this moment in time, dismantling the structure of White supremacy in the U.S. is necessary for both the safety and security of the Jewish community as well as the Black community (Belding-Zidon, 2020). Both Blacks and Jews benefit from eliminating White supremacy, and that must be a common goal as we move forward.

There is no better time to come together as minority groups than right now, in the continuing struggle with COVID-19 and the fight for BLM. According to Cohen (2020):

> Jewish involvement in the fight against racism and discrimination has been a central part of the Jewish American experience, and is also increasingly a defining aspect of its future, as emerging generations of young Jewish adults see their Jewish identity interwoven with calls to fight for justice and inclusion. (p. 4)

In a positive sign for the future, many Jewish groups have stepped forward to help support the BLM protests. For example, despite a history of conflict with the Black community, young Hasidic Jews in the Crown Heights neighborhood of New York City (U.S.) held a rally in June 2020 in solidarity with the BLM movement (Wax-Thibodeaux, 2020). While some Jews are concerned about the BLM stance on Israel and their often-contentious relationship with Palestine (Rishon, 2016), this needs to be put on the back burner for now, because, "If we expect people to show up for our pain, we have to show up for theirs" (Belding-Zidon, 2020, p. 2). It is the just thing to do. The bottom line is that, "If we Jews hope others will be there when we need them, we must be as sensitive to their needs as we hope they will be to ours. A key step is to realize that as a people we have not always been who we wish we had been" (Kulwin, 2020, p. 3).

As mentioned earlier in the text, there are many Jews of color living in the U.S., with diverse backgrounds, such as African, Latinx, Asian, Sephardic, and Mizrahi (Rishon, 2015). Since Jews of color have been found to comprise at least 12–15% of the Jewish population in the U.S. (Kelman et al., 2019, p. 2), it is essential for the Black and Jewish communities to come together. Cohen (2020) commented that, "Jews of Color often feel marginalized and excluded from mainstream Jewish life and, in many ways, also reflect society's overall struggle to engage Black Americans in just ways" (p. 4). The reality is that, "Black and Brown Jews face racism and invisibility in the Jewish community because they lack white privilege" (Love, 2020, p. 3); therefore, for those who are both Jewish and of color, it is even more pressing to confront antisemitism and other forms of racism head-on.

CONCLUSION

From my research, it appears that many Jews are prone to identify commonalities with the Black community, and they almost always fall back on the Civil Rights era as an example of the positive, strong relationship that exists (or can exist) between Blacks and Jews. If our individual and collective histories have taught us anything, it is that it is not that simple. While the latest spate of antisemitic blather from Black celebrities and athletes is upsetting and offensive to many Jews, it is an important reminder that we still have a great deal of work to do. I truly believe that Jews need to own up to the actions (or lack thereof) of our ancestors, from the times of slavery to the modern day. Hypersensitivity over BLM's antagonism toward the state of Israel must not deter our full-fledged support for all forms of engaged social justice. Katz and Lipstadt (2020) have stated that:

> To advance the cause of Black-Jewish relations today, the great challenge is for voices of compassion and mutual respect to rise above the prevailing din of acrimony, misunderstanding and distrust. Such voices should begin with a greater understanding of both Jews' and Blacks' complex, often painful histories – and how the past has shaped each group's collective identity. (p. 6)

In order to build stronger bonds and a deeper understanding of the Black community, both Blacks and Jews need to work diligently to discard myths of days gone by and accept the lived realities of each group as it is today (Morris

& Rubin, 1993). There is no more time for idealization and false equivalencies in the Black/Jewish relationship. According to Reid-Pharr (1996):

> In every respect these flare-ups help only to substantiate the half-formed racist notions that people carry about who we are…The work that stands before us, then, is precisely to work, to go beyond the practice of simply throwing a few good vibes in the direction of the opposing camp and instead to insist upon a thorough reconceptualization of both the ways in which we communicate and the manner in which we constitute ourselves as individuals and communities. (p. 147)

So, both Jews and Blacks need to begin to listen to each other and communicate openly and honestly in order to build stronger bonds between the two groups in the United States. As the old adage goes, "There is strength in numbers."

CHAPTER 4

HEBCRIT: A NEW DIMENSION OF CRITICAL RACE THEORY

INTRODUCTION

When my younger son was five years old, and we were living in a predominantly Evangelical Christian community in northeast Alabama, he told me that he felt bad about himself for being Jewish. Up to this point in his young life, his mother and I had never discussed issues of self-esteem and ethnoreligious pride. My son's early exposure to his Jewish faith was limited to a preschool version of religious school, "family services," and High Holiday celebrations at home. Since the nearest synagogue was over 60 miles away, attending services was a rare occurrence.

For my wife and I living as "Delta Jews" in the deep South in the U.S. (Cohen Ferris, 2004), it was (and continues to be) a daily challenge confronting Christian privilege. Here, we saw "Jesus Saves" billboards on the roadways, heard local radio deejays say prayers for "a day full of blessings," the invocation of Jesus' name during an introductory prayer at the annual university faculty/staff convocation, and "Jesus 2020" lawn signs posted around my neighborhood during the 2020 presidential election. For some, Christian privilege can often feel smothering and ever-prescient, but I avoided approaching the issue with my young son. I simply wanted him to be a happy child in kindergarten, but when I had heard that there were going to be Christmas activities for two straight weeks at his elementary school, culminating in a visit from Santa Claus, I was concerned. In the past, while living in southern New Mexico, my wife had visited my children's classes to speak briefly about Hanukkah so my boys would feel represented in school. Here in Alabama, we were informed by my son's school principal that my wife would not be able to visit his classroom and talk about Hanukkah – reason being that she did not want parent visitors in the classroom. This was simply unacceptable, so I contacted the Assistant Superintendent of the school district to argue my case for the opportunity to educate my son's classmates about his family's culture and traditions for this (minor) Jewish holiday. I eventually researched and produced a Supreme Court decision that

© DANIEL IAN RUBIN, 2021 | DOI:10.1163/9789004464087_004

stated that while public schools are able to celebrate Christmas, they cannot favor one religion over another; therefore, by denying my son the right to discuss Hanukkah, the district was in violation of the law. Finally, as a concession, the Assistant Superintendent allowed my son's teacher to read two provided books about Hanukkah and distribute dreidels[1] to his classmates.

I can only wish that that was the only bout of intolerance that my family and I have encountered in just the past few years living in the deep south. For example, my wife was accosted at a local car dealership for her "Coexist" bumper sticker and how she does not believe in Jesus as her lord and savior, an anonymous person called me a "kike" via an academic website, and on my first night of class at Jacksonville State University teaching a required secondary education course in diversity and multiculturalism, after I mentioned that I was Jewish, a student in the front of the class yelled out excitedly that meeting a Jewish person was on her "bucket list." It is nothing new for me to play the role of the token Jew (Altman et al., 2010) as well as the cultural outsider, but this had only worsened since my move to the deep south.

I tell these stories because Jewish Americans[2] are overlooked, not only as a minority group, but as a group needing discussion in the university classroom. Jewish people are also often unexplored in educational research in the United States. From exhaustive research over the past decade, I have found very few articles addressing Jews and multiculturalism in the U.S. Quite simply, Jews are often left out of university diversity and multicultural classroom discussions (MacDonald-Dennis, 2006; Rubin, 2013; Schlosser et al., 2009), especially in regard to the topic of antisemitism, or Jewish oppression (MacDonald-Dennis, 2006). The lack of focus on Jews and antisemitism is evident in several ways, such as the lack of available research pertaining to Jews and the multicultural classroom, the difficulty of getting Jewish-themed pieces accepted into multicultural journals (see Chapter 7), and the absence of Jews and antisemitism in major diversity and multicultural literature texts used at the university level (Kremer, 2001; Rubin, 2018b). For better or worse, Jews are also considered to be a "model minority" (Freedman, 2005), so they appear successful economically and educationally and stay out of trouble (Maddux et al., 2008).

HEBCRIT AND CRITICAL RACE THEORY

Critical Race Theory (CRT) emerged out of a legal movement in the 1970s called critical legal studies (Delgado & Stefancic, 2017; Ladson-Billings, 1999). These studies critiqued the intersection of race and the law, how the law affects individuals and groups in particular cultural and social contexts (Ladson-Billings, 1998), and how litigation from the civil rights movement failed to achieve significant racial improvement in society (Liu, 2009). Similar to critical legal studies, CRT seeks to both eliminate and transform unfair and unjust laws (Bell & Edmonds, 1993). The shift from CRT in law to CRT in education is primarily attributed to the work of Gloria Ladson-Billings and William Tate (1995) (Cabrera, 2018). The CRT movement is described as "a collection of activists and scholars engaged in studying and transforming the relationship among race, racism, and power" (Delgado & Stefancic, 2017, p. 3).

There are several basic tenets of CRT. According to Delgado and Stefancic (2017), they are as follows: (1) racism in society is ordinary and unacknowledged, (2) "interest convergence," or the idea that racism supports and advances the interests of White people, (3) "social construction," or the belief that the notion of race is socially invented, manipulated, and changes over time, and (4) the importance of "storytelling" and hearing unique voices of color. Ladson-Billings and Tate (1995) asserted that issues of race in U.S. schools was under-theorized and that racial inequities still existed in both schools and society, especially in regard to Black students.

CRT has been described as a theoretical framework that is based in radical activism (Rollock & Gillborn, 2011) and is committed to social justice (Solórzano & Bernal, 2001). Its purpose is to investigate and challenge the prevalence of racial inequality in society (Rollock & Gillborn, 2011) as well as other forms of subordination based on class, gender, and sexual orientation (Solórzano & Yosso, 2001). CRT has been adapted and modified since its inception in order to address racism in society and schools. Sleeter (2017) posited that, "CRT offers conceptual tools for interrogating how race and racism have been institutionalized and are maintained" (p. 157), and by doing so, helps break down racism and prejudice in society.

The use of CRT in education scholarship has grown significantly since its inception over two decades ago (Dixson & Anderson, 2018), and it has since become a major concept all around the world (Rollock & Gillborn, 2011). Over that time, CRT has expanded to include several theoretical offshoots, such as Latina/Latino critical race theory (LatCrit) (Solórzano & Yosso, 2001), Tribal critical race theory (TribalCrit) (Brayboy, 2005), and Asian critical race theory (AsianCrit) (Chang, 1993). The purpose of this chapter is to outline a new Jewish critical race framework called HebCrit (pronounced "heeb" crit).

HebCrit develops from CRT and has similarities in the fight against racism and injustice in U.S. society. The name HebCrit comes from the term

CHAPTER 4

"hebe," which is an antiquated ethnic slur aimed at Jewish people. It is hereby reclaimed and positioned as a point of critical strength. While CRT has been a very important framework in education studies, it does not go far enough in identifying and addressing the specific needs of the Jewish peoples. It does not adequately address Jewish persecution in the form of antisemitism, where Jews fit in the field of racial studies, and the complicated positionality of Jewish people in U.S. society. The HebCrit framework has five major assertions:

1. Jews continue to be discriminated against and persecuted.
2. Jews are a racialized group.
3. Jews, and their perception as White, creates invisibility and tension.
4. Jews' political and economic power is hyperbolic.
5. Jewish personal stories have value.

JEWS DEFINED

The Jewish people are comprised of three major groups: the Ashkenazim, the Sephardim, and the Mizrahim. Sephardic Jews are those whose descendants were expelled from the Iberian Peninsula (Spain and Portugal) in 1492 during the Spanish Inquisition, while Mizrahi Jews originate from the Middle East and North Africa (Jewish Virtual Library, 2019). When discussing Jewish people in this piece, I am referring to Ashkenazi Jews. Ashkenazi Jews come from Central and Eastern Europe, are the most populous of the Jewish groups in North America (Solomin, 2019), and have a light skin tone. Therefore, Schlosser (2006) posited that, "The Ashkenazim are…quite often, the face of American Jewry" (p. 426).

JEWS AS A PERSECUTED GROUP

According to Marable (1992), racism is defined as a "system of ignorance, exploitation, and power to oppress African Americans, Latinos, Asians, Pacific Americans, and American Indians and other people on the basis of ethnicity, culture, mannerisms, and color" (p. 5, as cited in Solórzano & Yosso, 2002, p. 24). Jews have a long history of discrimination and persecution in the U.S. For example, due to segregationist beliefs in major cities across the U.S. during the first half of the twentieth century, there were often restrictive covenants barring the rental or sale of homes to both people of Jewish descent and people of color (Jones-Correa, 2001; Silva, 2009). There is also documentation of economic discrimination against Jews at this time, whereby employers would often not hire Jews, so they were forced to open their own businesses. There was even a quota system in many office buildings as to how many Jews, if at all, could rent office space (Weber, 1991). It has also been reported that Jews, during the early 1900s, were often ostracized in their local communities by being turned away from joining country clubs and civic groups (Dinnerstein, 1994).

In the United States today, racism against Jews, in the form of antisemitism, continues to thrive and flourish, and it has become increasingly worse since the election of President Donald Trump in 2016. Research has shown that, "Trump has emboldened racists to express their hateful rhetoric out in the open" (Crandall et al., 2018). For example, White Nationalist and Neo-Nazi fervor was on full display during the "Unite the Right" rally in Charlottesville, Virginia in August 2017. Encouraged and invigorated by Trump's racist brand of leadership (Roberts, 2017), White Nationalists chanted phrases such as "Jews will not replace us" and "blood and soil" while marching through the streets with tiki torches (Rosenberg, 2017). It has been found that the Parkland (Florida, U.S.) school shooting in spring 2018 was at least partly driven by Jewish hatred (Cohen, 2018). It has been asserted that Trump, in his passive, indirect condemnation of White Nationalists, provided racists with unspoken support (Abramsky, 2018; Ioffe, 2018). Trump rallies were often filled with antisemitic code-words, such as "globalist" and "cosmopolitan," which did nothing but add fuel to antisemitic fervor (Abramsky, 2018). Ultimately, according to Haltiwanger (2020), "For years, white supremacists have looked at Trump's racist, xenophobic rhetoric as a source of encouragement. And some of the most prominent far right groups have openly embraced and endorsed the president" (para. 12). It must be noted that antisemitism does not just come from right-wing groups; it continues to be a growing concern on the left (Thiessen, 2019). Hirsh (2018) posited that, "Today's antisemitism is difficult to recognize because it does not come dressed in a Nazi uniform and it does not openly proclaim its hatred or fear of Jews" (p. 5). Antisemitic beliefs often emerge through the democratic criticism of Israel, which then transforms into antisemitism (Hirsh, 2018). People who view themselves as progressives are frequently critical of Zionism and supporters of the boycott, divestment, and sanctions (BDS) movement against Israel, often called the "new antisemitism" (Cravatts, 2011). Antisemitism can come in many forms, both aggressive and peaceful, and from all facets of the political spectrum.

Rising antisemitism is not just occurring in the U.S. It has been claimed that large Jewish communities in Europe are also experiencing a mainstreaming

CHAPTER 4

and normalization of antisemitism not seen since World War II, and this has led to many Jewish people living with a sense of fear and distress (Noack, 2018). According to Walt (2019):

> Anti-Semitism is flourishing worldwide...The numbers speak plainly in country after country. For each of the past three years, the U.K. has reported the highest number of anti-Semitic incidents ever recorded. In France, with the world's third biggest Jewish population, government records showed a 74% spike in anti-Semitic acts between 2017 and 2018. And in Germany, anti-Semitic incidents rose more than 19% last year. (p. 2)

In addition, the number of reported antisemitic incidents in Australia has continued to increase since records began to be published in the late 1980s (Gross & Rutland, 2014). In the United Kingdom, a record number of antisemitic incidents were recorded between January 2019 and June 2019, which was a 10% increase from the same period the previous year and was also a record high (Sherwood, 2019). Overall, a recent global survey estimates that at least one out of every four adults around the world (26%) hold antisemitic attitudes (Tausch, 2014, p. 50), which is incredibly troubling and concerning.

As it stands, CRT does not adequately address Jewish persecution in both U.S society and around the world and how it affects the individual. Therefore, there is a need for HebCrit and bringing Jewish animus to the forefront of critical race research.

JEWS AND THE QUESTION OF RACE

One of the apparent reasons for the lack of application of CRT for Jewish people is the question of race. According to Greenberg (2013), "American Jews have always navigated uneasily between religion and ethnicity, race and color. They have never existed comfortably within America's binaries" (p. 45). The question of Jews being a distinct race has been debated around the world for centuries. According to Levine-Rasky (2008):

> In Europe, Jews were historically classified as racially distinct, even abject. Even before the rise of the 'race' concept...Their racialization in Europe escalated. Jews' allegedly unethical business practices. Jewish colour, hair, nose, feet, speech, hand gestures and facial expression combined to reveal a class of people essentially different from the European norm. (p. 55)

The scientific racial study of Jews first occurred during the eighteenth century, and it was unclear as to which race they belonged; some scientists saw Jews as being White while others saw them as Black or possibly White with "Black features" (Efron, 2013). In the late nineteenth and early twentieth centuries, Jews were often considered to be a separate race (Fox, 2018; Kaplan, 2003) with a distinct physiognomy (Blumenfeld, 2006b; Fox, 2018). While this chapter does not go deeply into the study of "race science" (Efron, 2013), it is important to understand that there has been a great deal of research on the Jewish peoples and their malleable position on the racial spectrum.

In recent years, there has been much debate as to whether there is a biological component to being Jewish. While some scientists believe that there is evidence that there is a biological foundation for Jewishness, there are others who disagree wholeheartedly. Kahn (2013) concluded that:

> a certain number of people who currently identify themselves as Jews have certain genetic variants that indicate a high likelihood that they are descended from populations that likely inhabited the Levant[3] some 2,000 years ago. These variants are not necessarily exclusive to people who identify as Jews, nor are they present in all people who currently identify themselves as Jews. Even Jews who do have these variants likely have ancestors from other parts of the globe. Nonetheless, it is not unreasonable to assert that, based on current genetic testing technologies and theories of genetic variation, there is a high likelihood that many contemporary Jews have at least one ancestral lineage that leads back to the Levant. (p. 923)

This debate will continue as genetic testing methods continue to improve and expand over time, yet for now, a genetically identifiable Jewish race is still debated and contested.

In the United States today, Jews have begun to transcend the line between religion and race, yet there is a dearth of academic literature that discusses race and racism in regard to antisemitism (as well as Islamophobia) (Meer, 2013). Gonzalez-Sobrino and Goss (2019) posited that, "Racialization plays a central role in the creation and reproduction of racial meanings, and its inclusion enriches the study of race and ethnicity" (p. 505). Unfortunately, this lack of discussion of Jews and their racial positionality in U.S. society leads to an absence of critical conversations regarding Jews and antisemitism in the diversity and multicultural classroom. Scholars such as Nye (2018) have stated that race and religion should not be viewed as separate categories. They assert that since the identification of religion is often used as a

CHAPTER 4

racial identifier for groups such as Jews and Muslims, "it is misleading to see the category of religion as solely based on issues of belief and theology" (Nye, 2018, pp. 4–5).

There are an increasing number of academics who believe that Jews are now their own race. For example, Kaplan (2003) contended that Jews are a sociocultural race – one with a shared history, descent, and appearance, and this creates a common cultural reality that forms an important part of a Jew's self-image and social identity. Nye (2018) summarized the notion of racialization when he stated that:

> In short, 'race' and racialization are not about skin colour and genetic classification. Such bodily attributes are a part of the discursive and ideological power of the concept and practice of race, of marking and organizing social differences on ideas of difference that rely on such embodied distinctions. In practice, though, race is also embodied in social institutions and practices – the processes of racial formations – that are manifest in physical and social experiences such as law codes, segregation in housing, education, criminal justice, and healthcare, and in the experiences of people who are classified to live within such structures of power. (p. 11)

While some may still argue that Jews are not a separate race, but rather a religious or some other classifiable group, this is highly contested.

Today, it is believed that race is socially constructed (Blumenfeld, 2006a; Greenberg, 2013; Ladson-Billings, 2018), and Jews are not considered to be a distinct race, but rather, lumped into the category of being White (Brodkin, 2000; Fox, 2018; Levine-Rasky, 2008). Despite this perception, many Jewish people have difficulty considering themselves as White (Blumenfeld, 2006b; Greenberg, 2013). A reason for being seen as White is that Jews are often ignored because they are invisible amongst their White peers; that is, unless they wear religious identifiers (e.g., a Star of David) (Blumenfeld, 2006b; Schlosser, 2006).

It was not until after WWII that Jewish people began to gain access to many institutional privileges of being White in the U.S. They soon became one of the most economically upwardly mobile European ethnic immigrant groups (Brodkin, 2000). Jewish Americans were able to "pass" as White and integrate into U.S. society by assimilating their culture, language, dress, occupation, and physical appearance (e.g., hair and clothing styles) (Adams & Joshi, 2016; Gilman, 2003). They also sacrificed their close ties to their Jewish communities and practice as well as inter-group alliances (Levine-Rasky, 2008).

The question remains whether Jews are a race. Jews were seen as a separate race for centuries. Scientists are now debating whether there are genetic markers for a Jewish race. I believe that Kaplan (2003) answered the question best when he stated that:

> while Jews may not be a (bio-genetic) race, they are a (sociocultural) 'race.' Biology notwithstanding, the racial identity of Jews is a *cultural* reality, which forms an important part of their social identity and self-image. Like Whites, Blacks, Asians and other groups commonly designated as 'races,' Jews are popularly identified both by others and themselves as a group with a shared descent, history, and even appearance. (p. 81)

Due to the lived experiences of Jewish people in the U.S., I argue that Jews are a race and need to be studied as such in CRT.

JEWS AND THE TENUOUS "SPACE BETWEEN"

American Jews often find themselves in a racial quandary – vacillating between being seen as White and as Jewish. There are Jews of color from ethnically and racially diverse backgrounds living in the U.S., including African Americans, Latinx, Asians, and mixed-race Jews (Rishon, 2015), yet the vast majority of Jews in the U.S. are perceived to be White due to their light skin tone. Weinbaum (1998) theorized that, "Jews find that [they] occupy a liminal zone – [they] have consciousness of [themselves] as outsiders and experience being excluded by insiders" (p. 184). While it is true that Jews benefit from White privilege (Langman, 1995; Maizels, 2011), they have this insider/outsider status (Blumenfeld, 2006b) along the racial spectrum. Therefore, as Jews started to be accepted as White, they found themselves further separated from other minority groups in the U.S., even though they still were not fully accepted by White society (nor are they fully accepted today). Herein lies one of the great conundrums of Jewish positionality – despite vast evidence of past and present discrimination and hatred of Jewish peoples, skin tone has become a sole identifier of Jewish people.

As will be discussed further in Chapter 6, it is often believed that there is a Black/White binary in U.S. society (Chanbonpin, 2015; Goldstein, 2006; Greenberg, 2013; Perea, 1997). In brief, the Black/White binary is a paradigm that explains that racial issues in the U.S. only focuses on two groups, Blacks and Whites, and that racial identities are understood through this binary (Perea, 1997). Since Jews are light-skinned, they are placed into the

CHAPTER 4

White category, yet this is somewhat erroneous. In the Black/White racial discourse, ethnic groups are now grouped as being either White or as people of color (Biale, 1998). This is problematic for many Jewish people since they fall within this nebulous "space between" the Black/White binary. Living within the Black/White binary creates a tension for many Jewish people, and it is important that critical race theorists begin to explore this tension. Psychologists have found that the tension can exhibit itself in negative ways.

According to Ladson-Billings (1998), "Members of minority groups internalize the stereotypic images that certain elements of society have constructed in order to maintain their power" (p. 14). For Jewish people, this can result in what is called internalized antisemitism. According to Rosenwasser (2002), internalized antisemitism (also called internalized oppression) is when Jews believe the disparaging stereotypes and messages that are thought to be true by those outside of the Jewish community. This can result in personal feelings of hatred, fear, inferiority, isolation, distrust, embarrassment, marginalization, shame, and depression (Rosenwasser, 2002; Schlosser, 2006). Internalized antisemitism can manifest itself in various ways, from showing disinterest in Jewish culture and heritage to denying one's own Jewish identity (Langman, 2000). Schlosser (2006) asserted that, "It could be argued that every American Jew goes through the process of learning (and hopefully unlearning) internalized antisemitism by being raised and/or living…[in] the United States" (p. 428). I would dare to say that internalized antisemitism is a much greater problem in the Jewish community than anyone truly realizes. Personally, I have battled with this for decades, and I was unable to identify the feelings I had until I learned about internalized antisemitism through my research. Liu (2009) posited that, "A CRT framework provides a situational context for exploring the impact of race and ethnicity on students' self-image and interactions with others" (p. 9). It is important that critical race theorists begin to address the under-researched area of internalized antisemitism and how it effects Jewish self-image. These feelings of internalized antisemitism are also influenced by Christian normativity in the U.S. Therefore, due to internalized antisemitism, Jewish people are subject to feelings of shame and inferiority due to an unhealthy personal identity.

Internalized antisemitism is also evident in the minimization of one's personal experiences of antisemitism. In a study by MacDonald-Dennis (2006), he found that many of his Jewish study participants minimized the impact of antisemitism on their lives. In a recent research study of Jewish academics in the U.S., I also noticed this trend (see Chapter 8). Several participants mentioned their personal experiences with antisemitism (e.g., being called derogatory names, having pennies thrown at them) and then immediately minimized and dismissed the acts by describing them as "typical stuff" and "the usual sort" of things that happen to Jews today. There is no name for this type of minimalization of feelings, and it needs to be researched more thoroughly.

Race for the Jewish peoples has never been solidified; they were once considered to be a separate race and now they are seen as being part of the dominant White culture. Although benefitting from White privilege, Jews also possess distinctive traits (e.g., traditions, belief system, physical characteristics), which separate them from the dominant ethnoreligious identities of their fellow citizens (Gilman, 2003). By focusing on how Jewish people have navigated the tensions between their Whiteness and their Jewishness, the study of race will only become richer. Through use of a historical, anthropological, psychological, and sociological approach, CRT can better understand the complexities of Jewish identity and positionality, for it is much more complex than often believed by critical race theorists.

JEWS AND THE ISSUE OF POWER

The notion of power and who has it is a major facet of CRT. Therefore, for groups such as Blacks, Latinxs, Asians, and Indigenous Peoples, analyzing the relationship between race and power is essential for social change (Delgado & Stefancic, 2017). According to Feingold (2017), "The fear that Jews have a special access to power is as old as Jewish history" (p. ix), and even though Jews have been a minority group for thousands of years, and have been stigmatized, marginalized, alienated, oppressed, and discriminated against for centuries (Alhadeff, 2014; DiAngelo, 2016; Hollinger, 2004; MacDonald-Dennis, 2006), Jews are now believed to have an inordinate amount of power and control in political and economic realms. A recent global survey shows that antisemitic stereotypes of perceived Jewish power are thriving in Europe. They found that more than 25% of Europeans polled feel that that Jews "have too much influence in business and finance. Nearly one in four said Jews have too much influence in conflict and wars across the world [and one] in five said they have too much influence in the media and politics" (Greene, 2018, p. 1). This continued belief in Jewish stereotypes and falsehoods is disturbing.

While it is true that Jews "are demographically overrepresented among the wealthiest, the most politically powerful, and the most intellectually accomplished of Americans" (Hollinger, 2004, p. 596), that does not translate to actual power. In truth, if Jews were so powerful, having membership in a secret cabal ruling the globe, they would have had the ability to prevent the Holocaust from ever occurring. They would also be able to extinguish anti-Jewish discrimination and hatred. Feingold (2017) stated that, "Jewish power is revealed as a tenuous force unable by itself to control the events that impact on Jewish life" (p. 146).

CRITICAL RACE THEORY AND JEWISH INVISIBILITY

History has shown that Jewish people were able to assimilate more easily into American society than other racial groups after World War II (Goldstein, 2006). Though assimilation might have been easier, that does not mean that it did not come without a cost. Historically speaking, Jewish people apparently acculturated quite easily into U.S. society, yet they continue to pay the price for that success. Due to the Holocaust and a long history of oppression, many Jewish people suffered, and continue to suffer, from traumatic stress and anxiety, depression, as well as a determination to overachieve (Schlosser, 2006; Schlosser et al., 2009).

It has been posited that many Jews do not even feel comfortable allowing themselves to believe that they are members of a discriminated minority group. Jews are told by society that they are White; as a result, they are quite different from other minority groups of color. Deep-seeded beliefs such as these continue to be harmful to both Jews and non-Jews alike. A more critical analysis of Jews through a CRT framework has the potential to create true understanding and compassion. In reality, Jews are consistently persecuted and discriminated against in the U.S. today (Rosenblatt, 2020), and by not being discussed in the classroom, the Jewish perspective is discounted.

HEBCRIT AND COUNTERNARRATIVES

CRT recognizes that one's personal account (stories) is of great value in better understanding issues of racial subordination (Solórzano & Bernal, 2001). In order for critical race theorists to better understand the lived experiences of Jewish people, there must be a greater embrasure of Jewish counter-stories. According to Solórzano and Yosso (2002):

> the counter-story is defined as 'a method of telling the stories' of those people whose experiences are not often told (i.e., those on the margins of society). The counter-story is also a tool for exposing, analyzing, and challenging the majoritarian stories of racial privilege. Counter-stories

can shatter complacency, challenge the dominant discourse on race, and further the struggle for racial reform. (p. 32)

Unfortunately, there are few, if any, research studies that analyze the stories (or narratives) of Jews in the twenty-first century, especially as it relates to issues of antisemitism and internalized antisemitism. Personal stories of Jewish people, such as my introduction to this chapter, have great value, for they have the potential to "recount an individual's experiences with various forms of racism or sexism" (Solórzano & Yosso, 2002, p. 32). This form of reflection is already quite popular in Black studies (Ladson-Billings, 1998) and Latinx studies (as *testimonios*) (Alarcón et al., 2011), and they give great validity to the perspectives of people of color. There are very few such counter-stories for Jewish people, and they are necessary to give validation to the "space between" that many Jews find themselves. In order to legitimize the perspective of Jewish people in the U.S. and around the world, counter-stories can assist in giving validation to the lived experiences of Jews.

CONCLUSION

As it currently stands, CRT helps analyze and understand Jewish experiences in the U.S. For example, CRT helps explain how Jewish racial positionality in Whiteness is socially constructed and has changed over the past several centuries. That being the case, Jewish people have specific needs and concerns that are not addressed in critical race theories and frameworks. Due to misconceptions and suppositions, Jews are misplaced into a racial category of Whiteness without understanding the personal conflict involved in doing so. There is a need for a framework that assesses and confronts the overlooked concerns of the Jewish minority, and it is called HebCrit.

There is no doubt that CRT has been an invaluable tool in the field of education studies, yet it does not thoroughly address the specific needs of the Jewish people worldwide. HebCrit, in addition to CRT, has the potential to address increasing antisemitism, Jews' true place in racial studies, and the complicated positionality of Jews along the racial spectrum. It also allows for a greater theoretical complexity to better handle White identity. Both Jews and non-Jews alike benefit from the opportunity to discuss antisemitism and break down any potential Jewish myths and stereotypes (MacDonald-Dennis, 2006) that can potentially lead to the harassment and discrimination of the Jewish peoples.

Jewish absence in CRT negatively affects the Jewish people, for it is a constant push and pull between acceptance and oppression in which Jews

CHAPTER 4

navigate where they fit in society and how they still are in danger just for being Jewish. This is a very complex and difficult balance for Jewish people, and it is my hope that HebCrit can begin to explore issues important to the Jewish community and better connect Jews to other racial/ethnic/gender minority groups in the U.S. and around the world.

ACKNOWLEDGMENT

An earlier version of this chapter appeared as: Rubin, D. I. (2020). HebCrit: A new dimension of critical race theory. *Social Identities*, *26*(4), 499–514 (https://doi.org/10.1080/13504630.2020.1773778). Used here and modified with permission from the publishers.

NOTES

[1] Jewish spinning tops with a Hebrew letter on each side, used for game playing.
[2] For the purpose of this chapter, Jews are identified as those who are perceived to be White due to their light skin tone. Often referred to as Ashkanazi Jews, they are of Eastern, Central, or Western European descent.
[3] A geographic area that encompasses modern-day Israel, Palestine, Syria, Jordan, and Lebanon (Jarus, 2016).

CHAPTER 5

WHITER SHADE OF PALE: MAKING THE CASE FOR JEWISH PRESENCE IN THE MULTICULTURAL CLASSROOM

BACKGROUND

"White" or "Other," I asked myself several years ago while completing an online survey for an assistant professor position at a national university in the U.S. At that time, I must have filled out at least 50 of these voluntary self-identification forms, and I had never really thought about it before. I'm White, so I ticked the "White" box and submitted the survey. Later that evening, I heard on the news about another traditionally Jewish fraternity being vandalized on a college campus in the United States (Timm, 2015), which was the third similar incident in the previous six months. I began to think. I am Jewish, American, and have a light skin tone. I'm not Black, Latinx, or Native American, so I must be White. I mean, I've always thought of myself as being White due to the color of my skin. Right? Suddenly, a thought crossed my mind – how can I possibly be White in American society if, as a Jew, my people are still being victimized and persecuted by those who are labeled as White? How can I be White if many White people in this country still dislike and distrust me due to my religious and cultural traditions? Furthermore, how do I navigate the notion of Whiteness in my own teaching of multicultural and social justice issues at the university level? All of these questions swirled around my mind as I wondered why, during my doctoral-level university courses in multiculturalism and social justice, Judaism and antisemitism were never discussed, not once, in my four years studying curriculum and instruction with a focus on critical pedagogies.

INTRODUCTION

In the new millennium, multicultural education and social justice courses have begun to make inroads in university teaching programs across the United States (Chou, 2007). James A. Banks (1992), a leader in the field of multicultural education, asserted that multicultural education was "essential in today's ethnically polarized and troubled world" because it attempts to "close the gap between the Western democratic ideals of equality and justice and societal practices that contradict those ideals, such as discrimination based on race, gender, and social class" (p. 32). While I agree adamantly with the necessity for diversity and multicultural education (DME), the simple fact is that Jewish people are not being given due diligence in the DME classroom in the U.S. The lack of focus on Jews and Jewish issues, especially in the form of antisemitism, is evident in various ways, such as their absence in major diversity and multicultural texts used at the university level. In an analysis of several prominent texts taught in the field of multicultural education, such as *Multicultural Education: Issues and Perspectives* (9th edition) by Banks and Banks (Eds.) (2016), *Affirming Diversity: The Sociopolitical Context of Multicultural Education* (6th Edition) by Nieto and Bode (2011), *Rethinking Multicultural Education: Teaching for Racial and Cultural Justice* (2nd edition) by Au (Ed.) (2014), and *Multicultural Education, Critical Pedagogy, and the Politics of Difference* by Sleeter and McLaren (Eds.) (1995), there is no real discussion of Jews in any capacity. In *Teaching for Diversity and Social Justice* by Adams, Bell, Goodman, and Joshi (Eds.) (2016), Jews are only discussed on a few occasions in one chapter titled "Religious Oppression" (pp. 255–297). As seen from several substantial, widely used academic books, Jewish Americans are still under-represented, if represented at all, in multicultural education texts.

While many university programs in the U.S. focus on issues of racism, classism, sexism, and heterosexism, little, if anything, is presented about antisemitism, or Jewish oppression (MacDonald-Dennis, 2006). Cohen et al. (2009) asserted that, "many major works on stereotypes, prejudice, and discrimination have paid relatively little attention to resurgent anti-Semitism" (p. 290). As stated previously, while some texts do address the topic of religious oppression, the specific discussion of Jewish oppression and/or antisemitism is still lacking. It has been contended by Altman et al. (2010) that "Jewish oppression and multiculturalism do not fit into currently established analyses of racism and economic oppression (i.e., underrepresented minorities, people of color)" (p. 163). In U.S. society today, the term "multicultural" is often synonymous with "people of color" (Galchinsky, 1994), and since Jews in the U.S. are perceived as White (Altman et al., 2010; Greenberg, 2013; Singer, 2008),[1] they do not fit into the category of multiculturalism. Despite the previously mentioned increase in antisemitic acts in the U.S., the discussion of Jewish discrimination is still absent from most multicultural and social justice university classrooms (Altman et al., 2010; Langman, 1995; MacDonald-Dennis, 2006).

According to Schlosser (2006), "Judaism is a culture, a religion, an ethnicity, and a set of traditions that is embedded in Jewish people's expectations, belief systems, and family dynamics" (p. 424). Jewish people in the U.S. most often belong to one of three main groups: Orthodox, Conservative, and Reform Judaism, and each differs in both practice and philosophy (Levine-Rasky, 2008; Singer, 2008); therefore, American Jews are, in no way, a monolithic community (Bernstein, 2012). Jews, just like any other minority group, vary in social class, education, political affiliation, and religious adherence. This chapter does not argue that there are huge variations in Jewish identity; it attempts to situate Judaism and antisemitism in a multicultural context, which is often missing in DME education.

In this section, I will attempt to answer several questions: (1) What is "Whiteness" in regard to Jewish Americans? (2) Why are Jews not often addressed in university multicultural and social justice course discussions? and (3) How does a lack of presence in U.S. college and university DME courses affect how Jews view themselves and their place in American society?

RESURGENT ANTISEMITISM

As detailed earlier in the text, there has been a continual rise in antisemitic acts in the U.S., both in society and on K-12 and university campuses. Around the world, statistics show that there has been a resurgence in antisemitic activity. For example, it has been shown that, "In 2018, there was a 74 percent spike in anti-Semitic hate crimes [in France], followed by another 27 percent increase in 2019" (Rodan-Benzaquen, 2020, p. 2). In 2019, violent antisemitic attacks in Germany rose by more than 60% (Henley, 2019), and it was even suggested by government officials that Jews not wear yarmulkes (skull caps) in public for fear of attacks (Robinson, 2019). In the United Kingdom, antisemitic acts have increased for the fourth consecutive year, which is now at a record high. This includes a 25% increase in violent assaults against Jewish people (Sherwood, 2020). There has been a "'sense of emergency' among Jews in many countries, resulting from concerns over both their security and their 'place' in society" (Roach, 2019, p. 1).

In addition, attacks via the internet are growing around the world thanks to the deadly coronavirus pandemic (Schwartz, 2020). There is a conspiracy theory circulating on the internet that blames the COVID-19 pandemic on Jews, Zionists, and Israelis (Estrin, 2020). Unfortunately, it is close to

CHAPTER 5

impossible to document the specific number of hateful antisemitic messages that are posted and sent via the web. This is a new age of antisemitic activity where antisemitism, just like other forms of racism and discrimination, are hidden just out of view (Cohen et al., 2009; Weinstein & Jackson, 2010). Due to these glaring statistics from around the world, it is essential that Jewish people are discussed in DME courses on university campuses across the U.S.

THE NOTION OF "WHITENESS" AND WHITE IDENTITY

It is important to note that, "To write of whiteness of 'race' and to write of 'race' is to enter a conceptual and ethical quagmire" (Levine-Rasky, 2008, p. 52). Whiteness and one's place in it is a complicated, multifaceted concept based on identity, acculturation, power, and privilege (Giroux, 1997; Green, 2016; Levine-Rasky, 2008). That being said, in U.S. society "we have come to understand that a European, white-dominated system formulated who would be considered white, giving permission to some groups to move freely up and down the ladder of social hierarchy developed around race" (Beam, 2007, p. 210). For Jewish people in the U.S., this has changed a great deal over time. According to Green (2016):

> From the earliest days of the American republic, Jews were technically considered white, at least in a legal sense. Under the Naturalization Act of 1790, they were considered among the 'free white persons' who could become citizens. Later laws limited the number of immigrants from certain countries, restrictions which were in part targeted at Jews. But unlike Asian and African immigrants in the late 19th century, Jews retained a claim to being 'Caucasian,' meaning they could win full citizenship status based on their putative race. (p. 3)

It was soon after WWII, during the 1940s and 1950s, when Jewish people began to gain access to many institutional privileges of being White in America and soon became one of the most upwardly mobile (economically) of all of the European ethnic groups in the United States (Brodkin, 2000). Post WWII, Jews were not really seen as a minority group in the U.S. by the larger society; they were simply seen as being White (Singer, 2008).

The notion "that Jews are White is relatively new and provides the irony that Jews, who have a long history of being oppressed by Whites as a non-White 'other,' are now grouped with the same Whites who have been their oppressors" (Langman, 1995, p. 226). Given this information, I believe that an important question to ask is whether it is possible for American Jews to truly be White if there are those in the U.S. (e.g., certain race-based hate groups) who think of Jews as being non-White. Singer (2008) also problematizes this concept when she states, "How can a society so concerned with promoting multiculturalism still not see us as a minority? I may be white, but I live in two worlds, and neither one totally accepts nor understands the other...We remain a hidden minority amidst white privilege" (p. 51). Now, it is true that White Jews, unlike most people of color in the U.S., often "pass" as being White by their looks alone (Freedman, 2005; Greenberg, 2013) due to having a light skin tone and facial features. As a result, they have the ability to reap many benefits of White privilege (Green, 2016; Langman, 1995; Maizels, 2011), such as the ability to obtain high-paying jobs, live free of police harassment, and move to whichever neighborhoods they choose. It has been asserted that being Jewish is really a form of invisible minority status due to the ability to blend in, or "pass" as White, within the predominant culture (Schlosser et al., 2007).

The question still remains whether Jewish people in the U.S. are truly White. That is a complex question and difficult to answer. When Levine-Rasky (2008) contemplated the issue, she asserted that, "Yes, sufficiently often in North America on the basis of 'race,' but 'no' on the basis of the instability of this category. Are Jews privileged? Yes, sufficiently often in North America on the basis of social class, but 'no' on the basis of its social cost" (p. 53). Jews have undeniably benefitted and continue to benefit from White privilege in the U.S., yet they are still often singled out for persecution and discrimination. In truth, being able to benefit from certain aspects of White privilege does not erase past and present acts of aggression and oppression of the Jewish peoples. In the U.S. today, White Jews still confront racist realties, such as vandalism of synagogues, gravesites, and community centers; physical and online harassment and threats; as well as physical assault. In addition, as I will be discussing in the coming pages, becoming accepted in U.S. society in the form of White privilege has also come at a great cost to the Jewish people.

Some race scholars have posited that there is a "second wave" of White identity studies (Jupp et al., 2016; Jupp & Slattery, 2010, 2012), yet this new area of study is not likely to affect how Jews see themselves and others. Jupp and Slattery (2010) posited that:

> Identifications, in superseding identities and identity formations, recognize that historical and social contexts structure and call identities into being...identifications are interactive narrative processes through

CHAPTER 5

> which identities emerge within social and historical contexts; therefore, we read respondents' narratives vertically for change over time rather than horizontally as static 'types' or 'maps.' (p. 458)

For Jewish people, this reinforces the idea that identity can change over time – both within themselves and how they are perceived as a group; this notion of Whiteness is not set in place for eternity. Lensmire et al. (2013) also discussed how the issue of Whiteness intersects with topics of gender, sexuality, or social class, and how this changes over time. DiAngelo (2016) has asserted that "many Ashkenazic Jewish people don't identify as fully white because there are aspects of whiteness – for example, psychological freedom and freedom of movement – that they don't completely enjoy" (p. 104). In other words, while there are some privileges that White Jews are privy to, that does not mean that they receive all of the privileges of the White population.

It has also been recorded that, for over four millennia, Jews have been scorned, discriminated against, and persecuted all around the world. Jewish people have been hated for being a foreign, mongrel race, who have only been successful economically due to their conniving financial trickery and corrupt bargains (Freedman, 2005; Levine-Rasky, 2008).[2] Jews have also been perceived as being dirty, swarthy, unattractive (having beady eyes and big noses), and even diseased (Gilman, 1994; Segal, 1999; Weinbaum, 1998). Additionally, and probably most importantly, Jews were accused of being the killers of Jesus Christ (Freedman, 2005; Gilman, 2003; Schlosser, 2006). Brodkin (2000) contended that "whiteness is a state of privilege and belonging" (p. 182) and, "Race is not just a matter of skin pigmentation or ethnic background. It is determined by both individuals and their observers, and the boundaries of who's in or out of one group or another change constantly" (Green, 2016, p. 7). That being the case, another question arises – due to the great distrust and disdain that many White people have had for the Jewish people over the years (or millennia), how did Jewish people ever become White? In other words, how did Jews become accepted and thriving members in U.S. society if they were of such low moral and ethical character at odds with the prevailing belief system of White America?

I will not present an exhaustive history of Jewish people in the United States in this chapter, but it has been documented that classifications of Jewish people, depending on the specific period in American history, have oscillated greatly. Ultimately, "Jewish identity, or the way Jews understand themselves as a group, is complex and shifting, constituted by social and residential ties, friendships, community interests, a shared sense of history, and religious and cultural practices" (Greenberg, 2013, p. 35). History has shown that, in certain periods, White society has assigned Jewish people to the White race; other times, some type of off-White race (Brodkin, 2000). According to Brodkin (2000):

> the Jews' unwhitening and whitening were not of their own making. Rather, the movements were effected [*sic*] by changes in national economic, institutional, and political practices, as well as by changes in scientific and public discourses about race in general and Jews in particular. (p. 175)

It was not until after WWII, and the atrocities of the Holocaust in Europe (also referred to as the *Shoah*, in Hebrew), that Jews began to be considered White in the United States (Weinbaum, 1998).[3] Lensmire et al. (2013) observed that, "White privilege is not the cause of racial differentiation and structures; it is the effect of the socially, politically, and economically constructed system that we call race" (p. 421). This changing of labels was primarily due to Jewish people's ability to integrate into American society by assimilating their language, culture, occupation, dress, and physical appearance, such as clothes and hair styles (Gilman, 2003).

JEWISH SENSE OF SELF

For many American Jews today, there is a difficult negotiation between being seen as White and being true to one's Jewishness, whether it be based on religion, cultural tradition, or family bloodline. For many American Jews, there is balancing act attempting to negotiate two different, and often tension-filled, worlds. How Jews see themselves racially can be quite complicated (DiAngelo, 2016). As affirmed by Levine-Rasky (2008), "A poignant tension arises in confronting the attained status of the Jews. Jews are both Whites and racialized, both privileged and impaired. This ambiguity creates fear" (p. 61).

According to literature in the areas of counseling and psychology, this is a potential consequence of internalized racial oppression by the White majority in the U.S. Pyke (2010) asserted that:

> internalized White racism...emphasizes the psychic costs of internalized racial oppression defined as the individual inculcation of the racist stereotypes, values, images, and ideologies perpetuated by the White dominant society about one's racial group, leading to feelings of self-doubt, disgust, and disrespect for one's race and/or oneself. (p. 553)

CHAPTER 5

These feelings of insecurity due to prejudice and discrimination are also referred to as "internalized antisemitism." Schlosser et al. (2009) defined internalized antisemitism as, "The passive and/or active concealment of one's Jewish identity and feelings of self-hatred" (p. 56). These feelings have led many American Jews to hide amongst their *goyische* (non-Jewish) neighbors. Gilman (1994) posited that American Jews have internalized the various negative images of being Jewish (e.g., as pushy, penny-pinching, cheats), and by doing so, they have internalized the desire to maintain their own Jewish identity while trying to not actually be seen as a Jew, which would be much more widely acceptable than being seen as "too Jewish."

Not looking Jewish was, and is to this day, still a concern in the American Jewish community. Many American Jews keep their identity hidden for fear of what might eventually come if they are found out to be a Jew (Altman et al., 2010), so they often go to great lengths to avoid bringing attention to their Jewishness, even to the point of having cosmetic surgery. For example, this concern of looking "too Jewish" is reflected in the desire for rhinoplasty (Gilman, 1994). As another example, proper grooming of a White Jewish person's oft curly hair, more recently referred to as the "Jew-fro" (Gilman, 2003), is also necessary in order to pass as White in the U.S. Many Jews undergo this type of physical transformation just so that they can pass as being White in America, and thereby, be spared any potential harassment and discrimination.

American Jews often see themselves, not only as a minority group, but as those whose existence is constantly in question (Langman, 1995). Four thousand years of persecution has created a sense of internalized fear, one which "leads many Jews to keep a low profile and not call attention to themselves as Jews. Historically, being Jewish has been dangerous, and that legacy is deeply imbedded in the consciousness of Jews" (Langman, 1995, p. 228). This fear is understandable since Jews have been persecuted in almost every nation on earth and have been continually seen as the enemy (DiAngelo, 2016). During the Trump presidency (2016–2020) in the U.S., antisemitism continued to grow with the emergence of the so-called "Alt-Right" (Hayden, 2017). Many observers have asserted that Trump helped legitimize racism by expressing his bigoted beliefs out loud (Grigsby Bates, 2020). Specifically, Trump has also been accused of being antisemitic. For example, it was reported that Trump stated privately that "Jews are only in it for themselves" and "stick together" (Chait, 2020, para. 1). Therefore, it will continue to be that American Jews are the proverbial wolves in sheep's clothing. As long as they are seen as one of the herd, they are safe, but as soon as they are exposed to be who they truly are (or perceived to be by non-Jews), then they open themselves up for potential violence and discrimination.

In large part to the financial gains of many American Jews in the last half century as well as blending into all aspects of White society, Jews are often seen as a successful, "model" minority (Gilman, 2003). The perception of Jewish Americans as a model minority is erroneous and misleading, as is the case for all peoples considered to be model minorities. Take economic success for example. Despite what many Americans might think, the simple fact is that many Jews live in poverty in the U.S. For instance, it has been recorded that about 20% of New York Jews live in households near or below the federal poverty line (Eisner, 2019). As discussed earlier, the stereotype of the wealthy, financially savvy Jew is just that, a stereotype, which was practically forced upon them by the Roman Catholic Church (Muller, 2010). It has also been posited that Jewish Americans have made great gains in the areas of medicine, law, and politics in recent decades (King & Weiner, 2007). While some believe that Jews are one of the most privileged groups in the U.S. and are even viewed as elite (Cannon, 2014) due to their mainstream impact on the arts and sciences (Alba, 2006), that does not mean full societal acceptance. Becoming financially stable and passing for White in the United States does not equate a positive perception of Jewish beliefs and customs. Despite the commercial success of particular American Jews in the music and entertainment industry (e.g., Idina Menzel, Ben Stiller), Jews, as a whole, are still discriminated against in the U.S. and judged as being "less than."

Ultimately, being perceived as Jewish can have a negative impact on how one sees oneself in U.S. society. This was evident when, in March 2015, a gubernatorial candidate in Missouri committed suicide after rumors began to spread that he was Jewish (Bever, 2015). While the exact reason why this person ended his life might never be known, the smear campaign about him being Jewish appears to be a primary cause of him killing himself. This particular instance is indicative of the existing negative connotation of being Jewish in particular parts of the U.S. Just because some Jewish people have accomplished economic success and mainstream popularity does not mean that Jews are truly respected or accepted as a people. Being labeled as a Jewish person brings its own weight and meaning in society, and for some, it is hurtful and damaging.

EXCLUSION FROM MULTICULTURAL AND SOCIAL JUSTICE DISCOURSE

As mentioned previously, the study of antisemitism is not often discussed in the multicultural and social justice university classroom, and it is imperative that university students be provided the opportunity to analyze critically the stereotypes which are attributed to Jewish people (MacDonald-Dennis, 2006). Not being discussed in the DME classroom tells Jewish students, in a subtle or not so subtle way, that their experiences have no real importance and that they do not matter (MacDonald-Dennis, 2006). In addition, non-Jews are also given the message that Jews are not in need of racial/ethnic exploration and discussion as are other discriminated groups in American society and do not deserve the recognition as victims of discrimination and persecution. According to Giroux (2006):

> The university should be a principal site where dialogue, negotiation, mutual understanding, and respect provide the knowledge and experience for students to develop a shared space for affirming differences while simultaneously learning those shared values necessary for an inclusive democratic society. (p. 190)

Universities around the world can create the ideal environment to discuss issues involving all oppressed groups of people, including Jews. They just have to be invited into the dialogue.

While the notion of Whiteness is often associated with innocence and purity by the White majority, it actually stands for domination, oppression, and privilege (Giroux, 1997). Jews have been alienated and marginalized for thousands of years (Alhadeff, 2014) and based on current trends, racism and discrimination of Jews in the U.S., and around the globe, continues to increase. While American Jews comprise a very small percentage of the United States' population, they have a very distinct culture and language (i.e., Hebrew and/or Yiddish), as well as traditions, which differ from the majority in the U.S. According to Grant and Zwier (2011), "Policies and practices that do not take into account students' intertwining identity axes risk reproducing patterns of privilege and oppression, perpetuating stereotypes, and failing at…supporting all students' learning across a holistic range of academic, personal, and justice-oriented outcomes" (p. 187). In other words, properly introducing antisemitism in university classroom discussions of multiculturalism and social justice can help change the tide of discrimination and hatred against American Jews for this, and future, generations. Identifying as an American Jew is quite important in modern society, for it determines how one sees oneself, the society in which one lives, and one's ability to negotiate both worlds – White and Jewish. Langman (1995) asserted that since Jews are not often associated with being a minority group in the U.S., "it is easy for them to doubt the validity of their experiences as members of a minority" (p. 228). Addressing Jews and Jewish issues in the university classroom can impact positively both Jews and non-Jews alike.

It is quite unfortunate that, in this day and age, antisemitism continues to flourish both in the U.S. and around the world. In DME courses, there is a need for open and honest Jewish representation and discussion. In the university classroom, "Everyone's perspective is not equally valid when some are uninformed, unexamined, or uphold existing power inequities" (Sensoy & DiAngelo, 2014, p. 4); therefore, issues of antisemitism cannot be fleshed out without proper discussion and critical analysis in the classroom.

CONCLUSION

Antisemitism is alive and well around the globe. In the United States in particular, acts of antisemitism have exploded since the election of a new president in 2016 (ADL, 2017), and this trend has also continued on university campuses (Regan & Romirowsky, 2020). An effective way to help break down stereotypes and misunderstandings of Jewish people is by creating a dialogue about Jewish issues in the DME university classroom. According to Singer (2008), understanding of Jewish issues in education is important for two reasons:

> The first is lack of knowledge in the general population and the permeation of this deficiency. The second is misinformation which may be disseminated due to lack of knowledge and poor choice of resources. The biggest problem comes from people not even knowing they don't know. (p. 50)

Unfortunately, due to many reasons, bigotry, stereotyping, and internalized racism are held by both Jews and non-Jews alike. It is for these reasons that American Jews need to be recognized as their own unique group that continue to battle various forms of discrimination and oppression (MacDonald-Dennis, 2006). A positive and productive way to achieve that goal is to bring the study of antisemitism into the multicultural and social justice university classroom.

ACKNOWLEDGMENT

An earlier version of this chapter appeared as: Rubin, D. I. (2017). Whiter shade of pale: Making the case for Jewish presence in the multicultural classroom. *International Journal of Multicultural Education, 19*(2), 131–145 (http://dx.doi.org/10.18251/ijme.v19i2.1415). Used here and modified with permission from the publishers.

CHAPTER 5

NOTES

[1] It must be noted that there are a great number of Jews, both in the U.S. and around the world, who are not seen as White, such as Latinx Jews in the U.S., the Beta Israel from Ethiopia, and the Kaifeng Jews of China (Levine-Rasky, 2008). The focus of this chapter rests solely on those Jews who are light-skinned and thereby assumed to be White.
[2] In Europe during the 12th century, Jews only became involved in money lending because Christians considered the practice to be necessary yet inherently evil. Since Jews were believed to be damned already due to their rejection of Christ, this was an appropriate job for them (Muller, 2010).
[3] For a more expansive, historical analysis of Jewish people and the notion of Whiteness, I suggest Brodkin (2000), *How Jews Became White Folks and What That Says About Race in America.*

CHAPTER 6

NAVIGATING THE "SPACE BETWEEN" THE BLACK/WHITE BINARY: A CALL FOR JEWISH MULTICULTURAL INCLUSION

INTRODUCTION

There has been an increasing number of antisemitic attacks on Jewish people in the United States in the past several years. The most horrifying display of antisemitism in the U.S. was the October 2018 shooting of worshippers at a Saturday service in the Tree of Life Synagogue in Pittsburgh, Pennsylvania (U.S.). It was the worst mass murder of Jewish people in U.S. history. Exactly six months to the day of the Pittsburgh attack, in April 2019, there was another shooting at a Poway, California (U.S.) synagogue, in which two worshippers were killed and two others were wounded. In a recent study by the American Jewish Committee, it was found that, "35 percent of American Jews said they had experienced anti-Semitism in the past five years, and one-third reported concealing outward indications of their being Jewish" (Rosenblatt, 2020, p. 2). While it has been asserted in this text that Jews continue to be ignored in multicultural classroom discussions on college and university campuses across the country (MacDonald-Dennis, 2006; Rubin, 2013, 2017; Schlosser et al., 2009), anti-Jewish hatred proliferates as antisemitic incidents on U.S. colleges and universities increase at concerning rates; therefore, it has been asserted that college campuses are "a hotbed of anti-Semitism" (Phillips, 2017, p. 1).

To the detriment of all students, the inclusion of Jewish people in university DME course discussions is still greatly lacking. This chapter will address one reason why this may be the case – the "Black/White binary." It appears that issues of antisemitism are often overlooked since most Jewish people do not fit neatly into this duality. The Black/White binary creates a tension and ambiguous "space between" for many Jewish people, which puts their place in multicultural thought in doubt. This section will also address the potential "who has it worse" competition in multiculturalism as well as the harmful psychological consequences of a lack of Jewish acknowledgment in the university multicultural classroom. This chapter will explain the

© DANIEL IAN RUBIN, 2021 | DOI:10.1163/9789004464087_006

CHAPTER 6

case for Jewish presence in multicultural thought and academic inquiry in college and university education programs across the United States.

THE DIVERSITY AND MULTICULTURAL CLASSROOM

The diversity and multicultural classroom, as it is discussed in this chapter, does not refer to particular ethno-religious studies programs at U.S. colleges and universities (e.g., Jewish Studies programs). It refers to the study of diversity and multicultural education (DME) in the area of curriculum and instruction. Although there is no one set definition of multicultural education (Özturgut, 2011), it has been championed by prominent scholars in the field of education for decades (by eminent scholars such as Gloria Ladson-Billings, Christine Sleeter, Sonia Nieto, and James Banks). According to Banks (2016):

> Multicultural education is at least three things: an idea or concept, an educational reform movement, and a process. Multicultural education incorporates the idea that all students – regardless of their gender; sexual orientation; social class; and ethnic; racial, or cultural characteristics – should have an equal opportunity to learn in school. (p. 2)

In teacher education programs across the U.S., multicultural education is able to provide future educators with the groundwork for important issues of diversity (Jupp & Sleeter, 2016). While most minority groups are covered in such courses (e.g., Blacks, Latinxs), there are still some perceived gaps.

Researchers have found that the study of antisemitism in university academic programs is still relatively nonexistent (Altman et al., 2010; MacDonald-Dennis, 2006; Rubin, 2013, 2017). This lack of focus on Jews and Jewish issues is evident in different ways. For example, there is little to no discussion of Jews in any capacity in many comprehensive, foundational texts focusing on the study of DME that are often used at the university level (Rubin, 2017). In addition, Cohen et al. (2009) asserted that antisemitism is not addressed in major works on prejudice and stereotypes. Antisemitism "can manifest on an individual, institutional, or societal level" (Schlosser et al., 2007, p. 118), and it continues to be overlooked in college and university DME classroom discussions, which is problematic.

RACIALIZATION AND THE JEWS

Jews in the United States have begun to transcend the line between race and religion, yet there is very little in academic literature that discusses race and racism in regard to antisemitism (Meer, 2013). According to Gonzalez-Sobrino and Goss (2019), "Racialization plays a central role in the creation and reproduction of racial meanings, and its inclusion enriches the study of race and ethnicity" (p. 505). Unfortunately, this lack of discussion of Jews and their racial positionality in U.S. society leads to the absence of critical conversations regarding Jews and antisemitism in the DME classroom. Nye (2018) has posited that race and religion should not be viewed as separate categories, and since the identification of religion is often used as a racial identifier for groups such as Jews, "it is misleading to see the category of religion as solely based on issues of belief and theology" (pp. 4–5). For example, during the Spanish Inquisition in the fifteenth century, Jews were viewed more as a racialized group than an ethno-religious one, which had grave consequences (Hochman, 2018; Meer & Modood, 2012). Glauz-Todrank (2014) stated that, "For Jewish Americans and the scholars who study them, religion, race, and ethnicity make up fundamental components of American social location" (p. 303). So, while there are an increasing number of scholars who believe that Jews are now their own race, this is still highly contested.

In brief, Jews have lived as a minority group for thousands of years or at least since the destruction of the Second Temple (Floyd, 2006), and over that time, they have been alienated and marginalized (Alhadeff, 2014) as well as oppressed and discriminated against (DiAngelo, 2016; MacDonald-Dennis, 2006). It can be argued that Judaism is not just a religion. It is also a culture and an ethnicity with a distinct set of traditions that are tightly entwined between both family and community (Schlosser, 2006). It is for these reasons that I believe that Jews be considered a race of people, and since they are victims of racism and discrimination in the U.S. and around the world, they need to be discussed alongside their peers of color in the multicultural classroom alongside those who fall within the Black/White binary.

THE BLACK/WHITE BINARY

Scientists generally agree that there is no real biological basis for race, and social scientists affirm that race is a social construct (Ladson Billings, 2018). That being the case, it appears that in the twenty-first century the study of race in the United States falls along a Black/White binary (Chanbonpin, 2015; Goldstein, 2006; Gonzalez-Sobrino & Goss, 2019; Greenberg, 2013; Perea, 1997). In brief, the Black/White binary is a paradigm that explains that racial issues in the U.S. only focuses on two groups, Blacks and Whites,

CHAPTER 6

and that racial identities are understood through this binary (Perea, 1997). Castagno (2005) has asserted that:

> Many Americans ascribe to [the Black/White] paradigm because it allows them to simplify and thus make sense of a very complicated racial reality and that *some scholars narrow their discussion of race to Black(s) and White(s) and thus implicitly appear to accept the paradigm.* (p. 454; emphasis added)

According to Perea (1997), the Black/White binary is widely accepted by multiculturalists, and very few people even understand that they use this paradigm to assess race relations. It can then be inferred that many in the field of DME accept the Black/White binary (knowingly or unknowingly) and then decide, through gatekeeping, via academic journals, textbook creation, etc., which groups are allowed into DME university classroom discussions. Lozano (2017) stated that, "In higher education, it is the tendency to equate the terms 'diversity' and 'inclusion' with 'black' or 'African American,' which, for all intents and purposes, ignores other racial and ethnic groups" (p. 28). It has been suggested that other groups of people, such as Latinxs, Asians, and Indigenous Peoples, have difficulty fitting within the Black/White binary (Perea, 1997). For example, "Asian Americans occupy a space of contingent racial identity primarily shaped and defined by White institutions [such as the law]" (Chanbonpin, 2015, p. 647). Also seen as a "model minority" (Lew, 2006) like the Jews, Asians must navigate the notion of the Black/White binary in all of its complexities.

The Black/White binary is so important to U.S. Jews because one of the primary assumptions against the inclusion of Jews in university DME discussions is that Jews are seen as being White. According to Brodkin (2000), "Whiteness is a state of privilege and belonging" (p. 182), and since American Jews have undoubtedly benefited from White privilege (Langman, 1995; Maizels, 2011), they are no longer in need of representation and examination. For thousands of years, Jews were believed to be ugly, swarthy, diseased, shrewd, moneygrubbing, Christ-killing outsiders (Adams & Joshi, 2016; Gilman, 1994, 2003; Greenberg, 2013; Segal, 1999; Weinbaum, 1998), yet soon after World War II, like the Italians and Irish before them (Kelkar, 2017; Stapinski, 2017), light-skinned Jews were generally considered to be White in American society (Biale, 1998; Goldstein, 2006; Weinbaum, 1998). U.S. Jews were able to accomplish this renegotiation of social status by assimilating their culture, language, occupations, hair and clothing styles, and physical appearances in order to go unnoticed by their neighbors (Adams & Joshi,

2016; Gilman, 2003). Post WWII, skin tone alone became the determining factor for Jewish people being considered White in the United States. This is despite the fact that, even as a collective unit, there are a great number of non-White Jews. Data show that, "More than nine-in-ten U.S. Jews surveyed describe themselves as non-Hispanic Whites, while 2% are Black, 3% are Hispanic, and 2% are of other racial and ethnic backgrounds" (Pew, 2013, para. 31). While there are Jews of color living in the U.S., the vast majority of Jews in the United States are perceived to be White due to their light skin tone. Jews often go unseen amongst their non-Jewish peers for this single reason. Ultimately, the question of how Jews of color fit within the Black/White binary must be asked and explored further.

According to Biale (1998), "as Jews became economically successful, they found themselves for the first time in modern history as doubly marginal: marginal to the majority culture, but also marginal among minorities" (p. 27). In other words, as Jews started to be accepted as White, they found themselves further separated from other minority groups in the U.S., even though they still were not fully accepted by White society (nor are they fully accepted today). Herein lies one of the great conundrums of Jewish positionality – despite vast evidence of past and present discrimination and hatred of Jewish peoples, skin tone has become a major inhibiting force in their access and acceptance into college and university DME classroom conversations (Rubin, 2013).

In the Black/White racial discourse, "Ethnic groups are now homogenized as either 'peoples of color' or 'White' (whether they so identify themselves or not)" (Biale, 1998, pp. 26–27). This is problematic for many Jewish people. According to MacDonald-Dennis (2006), "One of the biggest difficulties in discussing Jewish identity and 'place' in the United States is that Jews do not fit neatly into established and understood notions of ethnic, racial, national, or religious identity" (p. 267). The Black/White binary just does not fit the specific Jewish condition in modern times since the reality of race in the U.S. has always been more complex than just Black and White (Martín Alcoff, 2003).

THE "SPACE BETWEEN"

How Jewish people see themselves racially can be quite a complicated subject (DiAngelo, 2016). I mentioned previously that U.S. Jews occupy an uncomfortable and ambiguous "space between" or "liminal zone" (Biale et al., 1998, p. 5), which exists within and without racial and ethnic categorization. It has been asserted that for Ashkenazi Jews deemed as White:

CHAPTER 6

> On many levels and for many of the historical, social, cultural, and economic reasons, maintain a 'bicultural' perspective within U.S. society. Our perception, historically from the margins and more recently toward the center, gives us our middle or insider/outsider status. (Blumenfeld, 2006b, p. 18)

In addition, most Jews in the U.S. can pass as White, thereby benefitting from White privilege, yet simultaneously, they possess distinctive traits (e.g., traditions, belief system, physical characteristics), which separate them from the dominant ethnoreligious identities of their fellow citizens (Gilman, 2003). According to Green (2016), "On the extreme right, Jews are seen as impure – a faux-white race that has tainted America. And on the extreme left, Jews are seen as part of a white-majority establishment that seeks to dominate people of color" (para. 3). Due to this back and forth, Jewish people's place in the White majority is a false narrative, and "On a more personal level, many Jews feel left out by multiculturalism, lumped as they are with those they have long fought to distance themselves from" (Greenberg, 1998, p. 78). In the twenty-first century, Jews are now, for all intents and purposes, considered to be members of the same discriminatory group that they continue to struggle with on a daily basis.

Jews exist in this ominous "space between" of race, religion, ethnicity, and color (Greenberg, 2013); therefore, in order to clearly and sufficiently address the lived realities of all Jewish people in the United States, the current Black/White binary in diversity and multicultural thought needs to be reevaluated to ascertain where White Jews actually fit in. Blumenfeld (2006b) has posited that "it is important for educators and others to realize that this racial divide (this binary) is itself a social construction and one that does not adequately take into consideration the collective history and psychic memory of the Jewish people" (p. 18). The Black/White binary only addresses skin color, and it does not address other potential factors that contribute to one's individual and/or group identity formation. Levine-Rasky (2008) asserted that, "Jewishness elicits a specific set of questions about Whiteness. Conceptualizing 'Jew' as 'White' is problematic" (p. 52). The reality is that Jewish people are often considered to be White in the U.S., and unfortunately, there are those who believe that only people of color can be subjected to racism and discrimination (Alexander, 1994). Invariably, the Black/White binary, which is a "one or the other" perception of race, does not work for the Jewish people. In a study by Blumenfeld (2006b), it was found that:

The majority of [Jewish] participants found it extremely difficult to position themselves on the racial binary (assignments) as currently constructed in the United States in which White is located on one side and persons of color (Blacks, Asians and Pacific Islanders, Latinos or Latinas, and Native Americans) on the other. To most participants, the categories Jew and Judaism not only confound the U.S. racial binary but also expose the fact that race as a concept is, indeed, a social construction (often arbitrary) reflecting historical, social, economic, and cultural contexts. (pp. 13–14)

Jews occupy this nebulous "space between" in the racial Black/White binary, which dictates societal acceptance on one hand and distrust and discrimination on the other.

Ultimately, the ability to claim which groups have the right to be discussed in university DME classroom discussions, thereby validating one's positionality as a victim of racism and discrimination, often feels like a battle for who has it the worst. While many Jews understand that, due to White privilege, they do not have the same struggles as people of color, it becomes an uncomfortable negotiation for representation. According to Gilman (2003), "Multiculturalism is…a space where the contrast between the haves and have-nots is played out. The more you can claim the status of victim, the stronger your case is for primacy in this world" (p. 128). Martinez (1994) described this type of competitive one-upmanship as the "oppression Olympics," and it is, again, a false narrative. Race is not a constant, all-or-nothing, state of being in society. As is evident from the historical and sociological analysis of Jewish people in the U.S. over the past century, racial categorization can evolve and change over time (Brodkin, 2000). Unfortunately, for many Jewish people in the U.S., if one is not distinctly a person of color, s/he is not accepted as having a valid claim of being oppressed and persecuted. In the case of the Jews, it is inappropriate that they are placed in the same category of Whiteness as Neo-Nazis and other racist hate groups (Langman, 1995). If Jewish people are still being persecuted around the world by those considered to be White, it is difficult to accept that they are now full members of the same White racial group. Somehow, that is exactly what is occurring in discussions of race and ethnicity in the U.S. today.

It has been observed that most American Jews do not view themselves as White (Greenberg, 2013), yet they find themselves in this "space between" the Black/White binary. Since the Jews' very existence is constantly in question (Langman, 1995), due to thousands of years of persecution and the memory of the Holocaust, Jewish people do not have the same lived experience that other White people do. Greenberg (1998) believed that, "The experience of Jews as simultaneous insiders and outsiders, both victims of and members of a privileged class, can strengthen multicultural theory by reinforcing the multicultural commitment to hybridity and highlighting the complex, shifting, and voluntary nature of identity" (p. 82). This analysis can never occur if antisemitism is not thoroughly explored in the DME classroom.

THE NEGATIVE EFFECTS OF JEWISH INVISIBILITY

Few, if any, DME scholars would contest the fact that "the moniker of black skin renders a different lived reality for darker-skinned [people] in a racist society" (Matias, 2016, p. 3). That being said, it is vital for multicultural scholars to understand that the lived reality of Black youth does not make the scourge of antisemitism any less real or substantive. History has shown that Jewish people were able to assimilate more easily into American society than Blacks after World War II (Goldstein, 2006). Though assimilation might have been easier, that does not mean that it did not come without a high price. According to Goldstein (2006), "While American Jews were often buoyed by their ability to move freely in White America, their entry into that world resulted in alienation, communal breakdown, and psychic pain as surely as it produced the exhilaration of acceptance in non-Jewish society" (p. 6). Historically speaking, it is obvious that Jewish people's relative ease of acculturation into U.S. society does not mean that Jews did not suffer or were free from discrimination and persecution. Due to the Holocaust and a long history of oppression, many Jewish people suffered, and continue to suffer, from traumatic stress and anxiety, depression, as well as a determination to overachieve (Schlosser, 2006; Schlosser et al., 2009).

It appears that the motivation to focus on antisemitism is not that important or necessary, at least when compared with the needs of other racial/ethnic groups. Sensoy and DiAngelo (2012) declared that, "Dominant group members tend to dismiss the voices of minoritized group members…as unworthy of consideration" (pp. 148–149), and since it is often assumed that Jewish people in the U.S. are protected from harm due to their cloak of Whiteness, they are not victims like people of color. Ultimately, through the eyes of some multiculturalists, Jews are simply unworthy of inclusion in the discussion of multicultural issues (Alexander, 1992). This belief, whether stated outwardly or not, is felt by many in the Jewish community. It has been posited that many Jews do not even feel comfortable allowing themselves to believe that they are members of a discriminated minority group since they are not people of color (Rubin, 2013). Simply because of the color of their skin, they are told by society that they are White; as a result, they are quite different from other minority groups of color (Rubin, 2013). Deep-seeded beliefs such as these continue to be harmful to both Jews and non-Jews alike. The invisibility of Jews in the DME classroom strips Jews of any potential for true understanding and compassion. In reality, Jews are consistently marginalized and oppressed in the U.S. today, and by not being discussed in the classroom, the Jewish perspective is discounted. For Jews taking DME courses at the university level also poses distinct risks. A lack of presence can infer that "[Jewish people's] existence is of no importance [which] exacerbates Jewish students' invalidation of Jewish identity and anti-Semitism" (MacDonald-Dennis, 2006, p. 276).

According to Blumenfeld and Jaekel (2012), "For members of minoritized groups and nonbelievers, [being other than mainline Christian] can result in low self-esteem, shame, depression, prejudiced attitudes toward members of their own religious community, and even conversion to the dominant religion" (p. 130). Jewish people sometimes have feelings of shame and inferiority due to an unhealthy Jewish identity. This is caused by internalizing antisemitic beliefs in the U.S., which is a Christian-dominated society (Schlosser, 2006; Schlosser et al., 2009). Many multiculturalists only recall Jewish persecution as occurring during the Holocaust. It is this select moment in time, a horrible one no doubt, that encompasses Jewish positionality in global society. Therefore, since the Holocaust ended over seventy years ago, Jews have surpassed antisemitism and have found their rightful place in the White elite (Rubin, 2013). As the data presented throughout this text attest, racism against Jews did not disappear after the Holocaust ended. It is alive and it is thriving in the United States.

CONCLUSION

It is important that college and university students in the United States are provided the opportunity to explore the concept of anti-Jewish bias in all of its forms in the DME classroom. This can provide students, both Jews and non-Jews alike, the chance to discuss antisemitism and break down any potential Jewish myths and stereotypes (MacDonald-Dennis, 2006) which continues to lead to the harassment and discrimination of the Jewish peoples. Jews occupy an uncomfortable "space between" in the traditional Black/White racial binary paradigm. Their absence in the multicultural

CHAPTER 6

classroom negatively affects the Jewish people, for it is a constant push and pull between acceptance and oppression. Biale et al. (1998) posited that "it is not only real and imagined anti-Semitism that makes Jews anxious about multiculturalism. As important is the consciousness Jews have of themselves as occupying an anomalous status: insiders who are outsiders and outsiders who are insiders" (p. 5). This is a very complex and difficult balance, and for Jews and non-Jews, if antisemitism and falsehoods about the Jewish people are not addressed in university DME classroom settings, then there is little chance for growth and understanding.

The lack of acknowledgment of antisemitism and Jewish oppression causes many Jewish people to feel overlooked, disrespected, and disregarded. Over time, the invalidation of Jewish identity can manifest itself in deleterious ways, such as shame, low self-esteem, depression, internal antisemitism, a feeling of invisibility, and even the desire to convert to Christianity (Blumenfeld & Jaekel, 2012; Schlosser, 2006). Jews are in need of discussion and analysis just like their peers of color, and it is the responsibility of all multiculturalists to address and discuss antisemitism and the complicated positionality of the Jewish people in the university DME classroom.

ACKNOWLEDGMENT

An earlier version of this chapter appeared as: Rubin, D. I. (2019). Navigating the "space between" the Black/White binary: A call for Jewish multicultural inclusion. *Culture and Religion: An Interdisciplinary Journal, 20*(2), 192–206 (https://doi.org/10.1080/14755610.2019.1624267). Used here and modified with permission from the publishers.

CHAPTER 7

THE MUDDY WATERS OF MULTICULTURAL ACCEPTANCE: A QUALITATIVE CASE STUDY ON ANTISEMITISM AND THE ISRAELI/PALESTINIAN CONFLICT

INTRODUCTION

A theoretical battle has been brewing of late; one which pits me, as a Jewish scholar, against those whom I support and champion on a daily basis. As an academic who researches Diversity and Multicultural Education (DME) in the United States, I am motivated to confront and educate those who attack others based upon race, class, religion, gender, sexual orientation, dis/ability, and national origin (see Rubin, 2018a). Yet, as I try to convince the multicultural education community that antisemitism, or the "unfavorable sentiment, attitudes or judgements made against" Jewish people (Moulin, 2016, p. 685) is still a major issue left unanalyzed in the United States, I am met with both resistance and refutation by my fellow educational multiculturalists. Alexander (1994) asserted that, "multiculturalists do not recognize antisemitism as a form of racism" (p. 63) because "their wise men have decreed that only 'people of color' can be the targets of racism" (Alexander, 1992, p. 65). From my research and personal experience, this appears to be the case. Jews continue to be left out of university multicultural classroom discussions (Langman, 1995; MacDonald-Dennis, 2006; Rubin, 2013; Schlosser et al., 2009) despite an increasing frequency of vitriolic antisemitic activity occurring around the world (Henley, 2019; Rodan-Benzaquen, 2020).

The classroom environment only becomes richer when a variety of cultures and experiences are included (Karatas & Oral, 2015). Unfortunately, researchers have found that, in university academic programs in the U.S., there is little to no discussion of antisemitism and of Jews being a discriminated minority group (Altman et al., 2010; MacDonald-Dennis, 2006; Rubin, 2013). This lack of focus on Jewish people and Jewish issues is problematic, for if the struggle against antisemitism is not recognized by popular texts, that puts into question the validity of the struggle. The reasons why

CHAPTER 7

antisemitism is addressed infrequently in the university multicultural/ethnic studies classroom discussion varies, yet, as mentioned earlier, there are several ideas that emerge from the research: (1) most Jews are seen as White[1] and therefore benefit from White privilege (Greenberg, 2013; Haynes, 2003; Langman, 1995; MacDonald-Dennis, 2006; Maizels, 2011); (2) they are seen as a successful model minority (Freedman, 2005; Gilman, 2003); and (3) they are accomplished in the fields of politics and finance (King & Weiner, 2007; Langman, 1995; MacDonald-Dennis, 2006), as well as the areas of entertainment, art, and the sciences (Alba, 2006; Gilman, 2003). It is here that I contend that there is also another reason why antisemitism is not often addressed in multicultural and ethnic studies programs – because of the negative perception of Zionism and the tension between Israel and Palestine.

ANTISEMITISM AND MULTICULTURAL EDUCATION

Antisemitism and Jewish acceptance are very complex issues in the field of multiculturalism. For some multiculturalists, it is a place where the Jewish elephant in the room is ignored, and when once identified, is told that it deserves the disdain that it receives due to its treatment of others. For example, at universities in the U.S., it has been observed that "students view Jewish issues as being solely about Israel and its treatment of Palestinians... [Furthermore], Jewishness has been associated with Israel, white privilege, colonialism and racism" (Jaschik, 2009, p. 2). Alexander (1994) asserted that, "The multiculturalist hostility to Jews expresses too the ancient tendency of majorities to bully minorities, especially minorities unlikely to hit back" (p. 64). And for Jewish people, due to their small population around the world (0.2%) (Pew Research, 2015, para. 1), it is easy to be abused as well as ignored. Therefore, it is imperative that antisemitism be discussed at the university level in DME courses. It is essential that university professors teach disparate perspectives and facilitate class discussions that support a wide range of opinions (Bernstein, 2012), for that is the only way to confront antisemitism on a local and global level – to critique, discuss, and analyze. According to Rosenblum (2007), "Every oppression is different, and every oppressed group deserves our time and commitment to learning what their specific experience is like, and how we can best support their struggle for liberation" (p. 7). Despite what some might feel about Israel's behavior towards the Palestinians, Jews in the U.S. (as well as around the world) deserve recognition in the multicultural and ethnic studies classroom. As mentioned earlier, antisemitism has only gotten worse in the U.S. and around the world. As an example, a recent study found that one in four Europeans still hold antisemitic beliefs (Rising, 2019). It is for these reasons that it is time that Jews be given the attention they deserve alongside their oppressed peers.

In the twenty-first century, there appears to be a tendency to ignore antisemitism due to Israel's interactions with Palestine, often seen as perpetuating the "'brutal,' illegal 'occupation' of Palestinian lands…[as well as] being a 'colonial settler state'" (Cravatts, 2011, p. 408). Consequently, many people believe that Israel is violating Palestinians' rights (Ghanem, 2016; Lasson, 2010). It is not my intention in this chapter to either justify or condemn the behavior of the state of Israel, nor am I refuting those who hold beliefs on either side of the argument. I believe that Bernstein (2012) said it best when he asserted that, "It is in no one's interest for colleges and universities to stifle critical but legitimate discourse on Israel" (p. 3). My concern is that the topic of antisemitism is rarely addressed in university DME courses in the U.S. due to the fact that there is an Israeli/Palestinian conflict – a conflict that portrays Jews, embodied collectively by the state of Israel, in a negative light.

Jewish people in the U.S. are, in no way, a uniform community (Bernstein, 2012). It is impossible to generalize Jewish peoples due to the fact that "Jewishness is a cultural identity, an ethnic identity and a religious (or non-religious) identity" (Rosenblum, 2007, p. 29). There is a wide variation in Jewish beliefs and attitudes across the U.S. There are many Jews who support Palestinian human rights, the use of boycott, divestment, and sanctions (BDS) against Israel, as well as a "two-state solution," but when an entire group of people is blamed for the actions of the few, as is happening with the Israeli-Palestinian conflict, that is clearly racist (Sheskin & Felson, 2016). Of course, it is possible to take issue with Israeli governmental policy and not be antisemitic (Sheskin & Felson, 2016). The two are not necessarily connected.

It has been asserted that racism and prejudice against the Jews has taken on a different form in the new millennium, with a focus on the state of Israel and its citizens, in what is now often called the "new antisemitism" (Cravatts, 2011). As mentioned earlier, campus antisemitism is still quite prevalent; in particular, there is a strong correlation between the presence and number of anti-Zionist groups on campus (as well as faculty supporting the BDS movement) and the amount of antisemitic activity on college campuses (Amcha Initiative, 2015). Data show that there has been an increase in anti-Zionist activity on university campuses across the United States, most commonly in the form of neo-Nazi fliers, swastika graffiti, and vandalism of Jewish religious objects (Rossman-Benjamin, 2019).

CHAPTER 7

This research addresses the potential systemic bias against Jews in multiculturalism and ethnic studies courses in the U.S. due to the beliefs concerning Israel and its interactions with Palestine. It is not my intent to create ill-will with my multicultural colleagues nor paint an entire group of scholars with a wide brush. The purpose of this chapter is to address the notion that the behaviors of the state of Israel, in some ways, are used to justify the ignoring of antisemitism in university multicultural/ethnic studies courses. The inspiration for this chapter came from the reception I received from a manuscript I had written exploring the issues of antisemitism, Whiteness, and lack of Jewish presence in the multicultural/ethnic studies university classroom (see Rubin, 2017). This piece is a result of the exploration of those personal thoughts and experiences during the manuscript submission process over the course of a year.

RESEARCH QUESTIONS

In this research study, my primary research question is: what are the participants' attitudes and/or feelings about the assertion that antisemitism cannot be discussed in a DME classroom without addressing Israel and the Israeli/Palestinian conflict? I also explored the following sub questions:
1. What are participants' attitudes and/or feelings about the Israeli/Palestinian conflict?
2. What are participants' attitudes and/or feelings about the Israeli government's treatment of Palestinians?

METHODOLOGY

This research is a qualitative case study presented through the lens of critical pedagogy. A qualitative case study "can be defined as an intensive, holistic description and analysis of a single entity, phenomenon or social unit. Case studies are particularistic, descriptive and heuristic, and rely heavily on inductive reasoning in handling multiple data sources" (Merriam, 1991, p. 16). Using a case study enables the researcher to address a wide variety of evidence, such as observations, interviews, artifacts, and documents (Yin, 2008).

I obtained my research data through individual, asynchronous, email correspondences with university professors in the U.S., well-versed (i.e. teaching) in the fields of multiculturalism, social justice, and Jewish studies. To find my study participants, I searched for academic scholars currently teaching at the university level, with more than ten years' experience in their respective fields, and holding a high academic rank (e.g., that of full Professor). I initially contacted, via email, four professors of whose work I found while doing research for a prior manuscript about antisemitism, Whiteness, and the lack of Jewish presence in university multicultural classroom discussions (see Rubin, 2017). From these original four academics, I inquired recommendations for additional scholars I should contact for participation; this is known as snowball sampling (Johnson & Christensen, 2012). Five scholars declined participation; in all, I interviewed six participants for this study. I decided on six total participants due to the anticipated amount of data they would provide for this study. I felt that six study participants would offer a great deal of information in order to thoroughly address my research questions.

Collecting research data via email has been found to be an appropriate method for a study such as this since it has been shown to yield both rich and insightful information (Hershberger & Kavanaugh, 2017). Email interviewing has many benefits, such as expanding one's access to potential study participants, saving time, reducing research costs, and allowing participants more time for reflection before answering (Bowden & Galindo-Gonzalez, 2015; James, 2007). The potential limitations of using email interviews can be misunderstandings due to a lack of social cues and rapport between interviewer and participant as well as potential delays in receiving responses (Bowden & Galindo-Gonzalez, 2015).

Since it is necessary to modify email interviews as compared to traditional face-to-face interview methods (Mason & Ide, 2014), the email correspondences took place over the course of several days from initial contact. The interviews were conducted in a semi-structured format. In this type of interview style, there are topics to be explored, yet the exact wording of the questions are not identified beforehand (Merriam, 2009). As such, the interview is more flexible and responsive to the line of discussion. In my initial email to the six study participants, I explained the research topic of antisemitism and a university Jewish multicultural presence and my concerns regarding feedback to a previous manuscript submission (discussed more in-depth in Results). I also attached two reviewers' comments in response to said manuscript submission for their consideration. After receiving consent to publish their thoughts, I posed the initial question intended to begin the dialogue: "What do you think about this? I would appreciate any insight you could give me." I was deliberately open-ended with this question since I did not want to steer the conversation in any particular direction. The email interviews ranged anywhere from three to ten email exchanges, depending on the study participant.

CHAPTER 7

For several participants, the initial brief question elicited comments that were insightful, articulate, and passionate. Some scholars also provided suggestions for further thought on the issues addressed in this study. For example, Dr. Goldberg wondered whether, "A Jewish presence in a multi-cultural classroom might require a conversation about antisemitism and its relationship to anti-Zionism? Even it [sic] you argue that it doesn't, shouldn't you address the issue at least in passing in your paper?" For these particular scholars, feedback was enlightening as well as supportive of the writing of this study.

Due to the nature of this contentious research, all research participants are provided pseudonyms in this chapter. While their thoughts are incredibly valuable, their strong, off-the-cuff opinions have the potential to be interpreted in both positive and negative ways by their colleagues and universities. Unfortunately, as happens quite often, their positions are provided thoughtfully and easily in confidential, one-on-one communication, yet these voices are not always found in the academic literature.

Table 1. Study participants

Dr. Feinman – Distinguished Professor of History at a small, private liberal arts college
Dr. Goldberg – Distinguished Professor of Jewish Studies at a public research university
Dr. Stevens – Multicultural Administrator at a small, private liberal arts college
Dr. Finkelstein – Professor of Jewish Studies at an Ivy League university
Dr. Maier – Professor of Judaic Studies and History at a private, research university
Dr. Holtzman – Assistant Professor of Near Eastern Studies at an Ivy League university

*Additional comments are provided anonymously by reviewers from a peer-reviewed journal in the field of multiculturalism and social justice in the U.S.

In order to thoroughly analyze the email interviews for this qualitative study, I used a critical discourse analysis (Fairclough, 2001, 2005; McGregor, 2003). Simply stated, discourse analysis is the study and analysis of how language is used (Barton, 2002; Hodges et al., 2008). This form of analysis is a valuable research tool in both textual and contextual research studies (Huckin et al., 2012) because it provides insight into the power dynamics of social interactions. Critical discourse analysis covers subjects such as racism, power, domination, and social inequality (Huckin et al., 2012; McGregor, 2003; Van Dijk, 1993), and it is particularly concerned with issues of power and control and the injustice and inequity which results (Van Dijk, 1993). During the data analysis, recurring themes emerged (McClaskey, 2008). I coded the emerging themes into specific categories for later analysis and discussion. They are as follows: antisemitism (veiled or intended), the need to discuss the Israeli/Palestinian conflict, and personal experiences with anti-Israeli sentiment, hostility, and frustration.

I used triangulation for general validity and trustworthiness in this research study. I did this to attempt to suspend any judgements, theories, and preconceived knowledge I may have had in order to help me see cultural phenomena in a different way (Creswell, 2007). According to Cresswell and Miller (2000), "Triangulation is a validity procedure where researchers search for convergence among multiple and different sources of information to form themes or categories in a study" (p. 126). This was accomplished through my layered interview process. I also had a professor play the part of a "critical friend," and he commented on my analyses, questions, and concerns as I moved through the process of writing this qualitative study (Heath & Street, 2008; Marshall & Rossman, 2006).

THEORETICAL LENS

This research is presented through a lens of critical pedagogy. For about the past four decades, the framework of critical pedagogy has been used by critical theorists and educators in order to analyze complex political, socioeconomic, and educational issues (Orelus, 2015). It is an intricate, multifaceted framework that has had a significant impact on many academic fields, such as sociology, education, cultural studies, and philosophy (Orelus, 2015). There are various definitions of critical pedagogy across academic literature, and I choose to follow the precepts explained by one of the leading theorists in critical pedagogy, Peter McLaren. He asserted that critical pedagogy:

> Constitutes a dialectical and dialogical process that instantiates a reciprocal exchange between teachers and students – an exchange that engages in the task of reframing, refunctioning, and reposing the question of understanding itself, bringing into dialectical relief the structural and relational dimensions of knowledge and its hydra-headed power/knowledge dimensions. (2001, p. 121)

By questioning the world in which we live – otherwise known as "reading the world" (Freire & Macedo, 1998) – new understandings of complex societal issues emerge through dialogue and critical analysis.

CHAPTER 7

It is believed that through education and the exchange of ideas between teacher and student, youth can begin to question the world in which they live in order to form a more egalitarian society. Critical pedagogy is centered in the process of critical thought, and it is based upon the vital and productive use of critique (McLaren, 2005). Ultimately, "[Critical pedagogy] is a powerful philosophical tradition that has attempted to bring the most formidable political and philosophical principles of a radical social theory to bear upon the education of oppressed communities" (Darder, 2015, p. xiii). In this study, critical pedagogy supports the critical assessment of Zionism and the tenuous relationship of Jews and multicultural thought in the university setting.

In addition, critical pedagogy addresses improvement of societal inequalities, inequity and exploitation of power, the repression of the masses by those in power (i.e., based on wealth and race), and how the omission of those particular groups in education can be addressed in schools (Darder et al., 2016; Keesing-Styles, 2003; Shudak, 2014). According to Aliakbari1 and Faraji (2011), "it can be said that [critical pedagogy] challenges any form of domination, oppression and subordination with the goal of emancipating oppressed or marginalized people" (p. 77). Exploring the issues of power and oppression is essential in this study due to the continuing Israeli/Palestinian conflict. Furthermore, critical pedagogy assists in answering the question of whether Jewish people continue to be oppressed and/or marginalized in U.S. society due to the actions of Israel.

ZIONISM AND THE ISRAELI/PALESTINIAN CONFLICT

For the purpose of this study, it is important to define Zionism as well as briefly explain the Israeli-Palestinian conflict. Zionism can be defined simply as the return of the Jewish people to "the promised land" in Palestine (Ashkar, 2015, p. 67). This process resulted in the forming of the state of Israel in 1948. Although in no way an exhaustive explanation of the struggle between Israelis and Palestinians, the conflict can be explained as a battle for contested land (i.e., the West Bank and Gaza Strip) (Rosenblum, 2007; Salem, 2014) as well as a struggle due to Israel's lack of recognition of Palestinian statehood (Friedman, 2016). In addition, according to Nicholson (2016), "Living with conflict has been a core reality for more than 60 years since the State of Israel was declared on land that was contested by the indigenous mostly non-Jewish population, 80% of whom were displaced elsewhere" (p. 5). As is evident, the issues surrounding Israeli-Palestinian tension have a long and checkered history. The point for this analysis is that there is a deeply rooted conflict between the two groups of peoples. This conflict affects how Israelis, and Jews as a whole, are represented in DME courses and treated on university campuses across the U.S. (Amcha Initiative, 2015).

RESULTS

The seed for this research was planted during the submission process for an article I authored titled "Whiter Shade of Pale: Making the Case for Jewish Presence in the Multicultural Classroom." The piece had been rejected six times from various multicultural, peer-reviewed journals, based in both the U.S. and the U.K., and each time, I found that the feedback was completely nondescript and blunt in its rejection. Due to the relative ease and success of prior publications, I became curious as to the rationale for the large amount of rejections that this manuscript had received (i.e., my critical thought process had not changed nor had my writing style and execution). I began to wonder if the topic of antisemitism was just not an issue that these journals found valuable or desirous. My theory became solidified upon receiving rejection number seven.

The detailed feedback from a peer-reviewed, U.S. multicultural journal were both concerning and cause for reflection. As seen from the words of the two reviewers, both considered by the journal to be "experts in multicultural studies" as well as performing "extensive teaching and research within the field of Jewish Studies (Reviewer 1)" (Journal Associate Editor, personal communication, August 3, 2016), the predominant concern with the piece was that I did not address the Israeli-Palestinian conflict in my analysis of university multiculturalism courses. According to Reviewer 1:

> Anyone who teaches on a US college campus today knows that Israeli policies towards the Palestinian people are a major social justice and human rights issue, and a flash point for debates over anti-Semitism. Critics of Israel see the Jewish people as a hegemonic, privileged colonizing power co-extensive with other white imperialist empires. Defenders of Israel see criticisms of its policies as just more anti-Semitism. I don't know how you introduce anti-Semitism and Judaism into today's multicultural curriculum without taking up these issues. The author's failure to address this subject and to outline how s/he would deal with it disqualifies the essay from publication in its current form. (Manuscript reviewer for peer-reviewed U.S. journal, July 2016)

Reviewer 2 had a quite similar take on the issue:

CHAPTER 7

> I would encourage the author to delve deeper into the implications of the role of Zionist racism in modern US Jewish identity. That is, approximately 40% of Jewish Americans identify in some way with the state of Israel, and this is an important and contentious issue when it comes to Islamaphobia, and Zionist racism, especially on college campuses with the rise of Islamaphobic Zionist organizations. (Manuscript reviewer for peer-reviewed U.S. journal, July 2016)

This unified response regarding the lack of discussion of the Israeli-Palestinian conflict was concerning for several reasons. First of all, I do not believe that one has to address Palestine in an article critiquing the notion of Jewish Whiteness and the lack of Jewish representation in the American university DME classroom. In a global discussion of Israel, antisemitism, and Zionism, the treatment of Palestinians is an important topic to discuss as a social justice issue, yet the need to discuss it in relation to American Jews is debatable. There are those who believe that, "Claims that criticism of Israel stems from anti-Semitism not only relieves Israelis of responsibility for anything except their own protection, but can also be used to justify repression and delegitimize critics, even Jewish ones" (Scham, 2015, p. 114). It is certainly understandable that a claim of antisemitism can be used as a method to deflect criticism, and the Reviewers' grounds for rejecting the manuscript end up supporting the manuscript's initial thesis (i.e., the lack of antisemitic analysis in university multiculturalism courses). Consequently, I reached out to experts in the areas of antisemitism, history, and multiculturalism to provide further insight into my beliefs regarding the manuscript's rejection and the notion that Jews cannot be discussed in the context of U.S. multiculturalism without addressing the Israeli-Palestinian conflict.

I first approached Dr. Goldberg, a Distinguished Professor of Jewish Studies, in order to get his opinion about the Reviewers' comments and the issues they address. He posited that the "reviewer's rhetoric" (Reviewer 1) did sound antisemitic because "when someone can't talk about the Jews outside of Israel without bringing [the Israeli-Palestinian] issue in, you know you're dealing with anti-Semitism." Therefore, according to Dr. Goldberg, the inability to separate U.S. antisemitism from the treatment of Palestinians in a Middle Eastern country is troublesome, indeed. In support of the Reviewers' comments, Dr. Goldberg did assert that when discussing "Jews within the American multicultural context [one] can't ignore Israel altogether, although certainly not in the polemical sense intended by [Reviewer 1]" (personal communication, August 5, 2016). In other words, Dr. Goldberg did believe that it is important to address Israel since it is tied to the Jewish American experience yet not in the way asserted by Reviewer 1.

Dr. Stevens, a multicultural administrator at a small, private liberal arts college, took issue with the comments from both Reviewers and found them to be quite insulting. He stated that, "I have come across this issue so often and really struggle with it. It is really frustrating that Jews are forced by many to have to think about the actions of Israel, no matter their relationship to the country" (Dr. Stevens, personal communication, August 3, 2016). Dr. Stevens did not feel that the Reviewers were insinuating that Jews deserve to be the victims of antisemitism due to Israel's actions. Unfortunately, he had met university colleagues personally who did hold those racist thoughts, though. Dr. Stevens understands and agrees that, when addressing U.S. Jews and antisemitism, the Israeli-Palestinian conflict is an important issue to identify and explain how the multiculturalist might address it in the classroom. Unfortunately, it is still quite frustrating that we, as Jewish scholars in the U.S., feel bound to do so.

When approached about participating in this study, Dr. Feinman, a Distinguished Professor of History, felt compelled to contribute. She explained how she was concerned about the Reviewers' possible political agenda. Dr. Feinman asserted that:

> It's one thing to raise a question about why you don't address the Palestine question. Fair enough, although you will have an answer. But the tone, vehemence, etc. makes the whole thing much more suspicious. Even if you agree (as I actually do) that many Israeli actions against Palestinians are reprehensible, it has nothing to do with Jews as a group. It's exactly this elision in the comments between Israel and Jews that is anti-Semitic. I don't label all Catholics as child molesters. (Personal communication, August 10, 2016)

This is a key point to the argument that some multiculturalists appear to ignore the discussion of antisemitism in university multiculturalism and diversity courses – that the perceived negative behavior of Israeli Jews speaks to the behavior of *all* Jews. By doing so, antisemitism is ignored due to the behavior of the Jewish peoples, as if they are one, unified collective. As stated earlier, there are many scholars who believes that it is perfectly acceptable to be critical of Israel, yet it is not acceptable to do so with an entire group of people, such as the Jews.

When asked her thoughts about the topic of multiculturalism and how perception is affected by the Israeli-Palestinian conflict, Dr. Finkelstein, a

CHAPTER 7

professor of Jewish Studies, had strong feelings. She stated that she was upset because the Reviewers' "obnoxious rejection" appears to "reflect a pretty widespread attitude. Many of my colleagues would agree with the sentiments, even if they would not express them openly" (personal communication, August 12, 2016). Herein lies my concern – that there are negative and pervasive feeling about Jews, Israel, and antisemitism, yet they are rarely spoken out in the open. I have found that having people speak up, honestly, about their critical beliefs of Jewish people, even anonymously, is difficult to come by.

Dr. Maier, a Professor of Judaic Studies and History, provided further insight into the discussion. She offered a detailed rationale as to why Jews and antisemitism might be missing from the multicultural education discussion. Dr. Maier theorized that:

> [Multiculturalists] might rightly say (although I do not agree with the premise) that persecution of the Jews was a matter of the past, it happened and is over. Jews now control a state, with a powerful army, a nuclear bomb, etc., and they cannot claim persecution. Therefore, they do not fit the [requirements] to be included in the multicultural category. They have achieved and are not outsiders, which is essentially what multiculturalism says is the issue with African Americans, Latinos, etc. (Personal communication August 14, 2016)

Even though Jews comprise only 2% of the total U.S. population, they are somehow not seen as a minority group needing acknowledgment in multicultural/ethnic studies discourse. In reality, "No one could argue that the trauma of past [Jewish] oppression continues to reverberate and that no matter how much clout, power, and 'insiderness' Jews have, they carry the legacy of trauma with them" (Dr. Maier, personal communication, August 14, 2016).

DISCUSSION

Manuscripts can be rejected from academic journals for a plethora of reasons. The issue here was not the rejection itself, but rather, why the manuscript was rejected from several multicultural and ethnic studies journals and what deeper meaning this held (and continues to hold) for me, as both a Jewish scholar and as a multiculturalist. The reviewers' critique of the manuscript solidified a suspicion I had held about the discussion of antisemitism in the university multicultural classroom, even though it is not addressed in academic literature. Based on the thoughts of several prominent scholars across the U.S., the Reviewers' critique appeared to support the idea that antisemitism is not often covered in the multicultural classroom due to the perception of Israel and the Israeli-Palestinian conflict. For that reason, issues relating to Jewish peoples and antisemitism need to be discussed critically in university multicultural and ethnic studies programs.

The study of antisemitism regarding U.S. Jews, and all Jews outside of Israel, appears to be tightly connected with the Israeli/Palestinian conflict. While some may assert that the treatment of the Palestinians by Israel does not factor into antisemitism, many students and teachers see a link. Caro (2015) stated that:

> The anti-Semitism of the new millennium has new sources, such as the growth of extreme right movements represented by European populism; the persistence of a radical leftist speech with populist elements, as is shown by some Latin American cases; increase of Muslim presence in Europe and the US; and persistent economic crisis. However, all these sources use the Israeli-Palestinian conflict as a propitious element to express anti-Semitism and anti-Zionism, which operate in a related and indiscriminate manner, blaming Israel and the Jews for Palestine problem. (p. 291)

Dr. Holtzman, an Assistant Professor of Near Eastern Studies, echoed these sentiments. He queried:

> Is [Reviewer 2] calling upon you to answer for Israeli policies vis a vis the Palestinians? …Or does s/he expect American Jewish students to do so? Is the idea that to have a legitimate place in the multicultural classroom one must (be able to) justify the actions of everyone with whom one is willingly or unwillingly associated? If so, one wonders: who exactly is left in that classroom? (Personal communication, August 14, 2016)

This is a very important point because U.S. Jews cannot be held responsible to explain the position of the Israeli government in their conflict with the Palestinians. They can only speak towards their own lived experience in the U.S. and the antisemitism they may confront in their own lives. Antisemitism exists and has existed for thousands of years, and this twenty-first century rationale of ignored antisemitism (or a "new antisemitism"), due to the Israeli/Palestinian conflict, is misplaced. Dr. Feinman added that:

> [The Reviewers' comments] reads more like, 'A nation of Jewish people is acting badly. That has to be addressed when we address anti-Semitism.'

CHAPTER 7

> Maybe it's more like saying any discussion of Arab American prejudice has to take into account the horrific abuses of ISIS. Yes, maybe, but exactly in the opposite way – ISIS leads to unjustified bigotry against Arab Americans or Muslims. [Reviewer 1] seems to be saying that because ISIS is bad, anti-Arab sentiment is somehow legitimized or must be addressed in that sense. (Personal communication, August 10, 2016)

In other words, Dr. Feinman asked whether U.S. Jews should be condemned due to the actions of the Israeli government. The negative actions of a particular sect do not legitimize hatred toward that group as a whole.

As stated several times in the study participants' responses, the Israeli government's behavior towards Palestinians is concerning, and to some, flat-out wrong. Israel has shown to be less than positive in its treatment of Palestinian peoples for decades as evidenced by:

> The demolition of legally unrecognized Palestinian houses and villages in the Occupied Territories and pre-1967 borders; the deferral of any substantive Palestinian governmental authority over lands claimed by Israel; the denial of, or highly constricted access to, vital resources, such as water; and the denial of the ability of exiled Palestinians to return for fear they will reclaim their lands. (Rifkin, 2017, pp. 27–28)

As a response to the actions of the Israeli government, Palestinian violence, in the form of bombings and knife attacks of Jewish Israeli civilians (in what is often referred to as "lone wolf" attacks), continue at significant rates (Beaumont, 2016). As is apparent from the recent mass killing of Palestinians protesting the U.S. embassy's move to Jerusalem (Maza, 2018), the Israeli and Palestinian struggle is as contentious as ever. This cycle of aggression has occurred for decades now, and it does not appear to be ending any time soon. Despite the horrible violence between the Palestinians and the Israelis, "People fail to remember that only two generations ago the Jews were among the most powerless and oppressed people in the world and that reality was a major reason for Zionism" (Dr. Goldberg, personal communication, August 5, 2016). It must be remembered that the Jewish state of Israel was created *as a result of* constant Jewish persecution, not because of it.

CONCLUSION

As a Jewish multiculturalist, I find myself becoming increasingly frustrated fighting for a Jewish presence in the multicultural academic community. As affirmed by some of the study participants, whether spoken aloud or behind closed doors, there is a strong belief that Jews do not need, or are not worthy, of being represented in the university multicultural/ethnic studies classroom. This needs to change.

I undertook this qualitative study due to the repeated rejection of a Jewish-themed piece I had written and the suspicions I felt due to the lack of acceptance of my assertion that Jewish people need representation in the university DME classroom. These feelings were solidified upon receiving feedback from yet another round of rejections. I believed that I was onto something – that many multiculturalists simply do not believe that Jews deserve representation as a racial/ethnic minority group due to the actions of the Israeli government. Unfortunately, there was nothing in the literature to substantiate my suspicions. Therefore, I had to begin the line of research myself. As a result, I created this qualitative case study that analyzed the thoughts and feelings of scholars in the fields of history, Middle Eastern Studies, Judaism, and multiculturalism through email interviews. A lens of critical pedagogy was used to analyze the data as it has direct connection with multicultural education. Several important themes emerged in the study: antisemitism (veiled or intended), the need to discuss the Israeli/Palestinian conflict, personal experiences with anti-Israeli sentiment, hostility, and frustration.

The data revealed that educational multiculturalists often ignore the topic of antisemitism in public and private university ethnic studies and multiculturalism courses due to the Israel-Palestinian conflict and the perceived behavior of the Israeli government. According to Caro (2015):

> Anti-Semitism appears related largely, though not exclusively, with the Israeli Palestinian conflict, showing that much of the anti-Semitic incidents recorded in the last decade and a half are linked to the Palestinian cause, and specifically to the Second Intifada as well as operations carried out by Israel in the Gaza Strip. (p. 304)

Several of the study participants stated that they had been witness to negative comments regarding Jews and Israel on their own university campuses. Unfortunately, comments like these are rarely made on record, so there is little opportunity to address and explore this type of deeply hidden antisemitic belief.

The study participants also elaborated on the forced connection between Jews in the U.S. and the actions of Israel as being unfair and potentially perceived as antisemitic. As a result, even though several participants believed that the actions of Israel are unacceptable in regard to the Palestinians, they

CHAPTER 7

did not feel that this justifies the large-scale generalization about Jewish people in the United States.

IMPLICATIONS

It is imperative that all educational multiculturalists, not just in the United States, but around the globe, address their own personal beliefs of who belongs under the umbrella of multiculturalism. Antisemitism is not only an issue effecting Jews in the U.S.; this is a global concern. It has been reported that there are growing antisemitic feelings around the world, which has resulted in a lived reality of fear for many Jews (Noack, 2018). In order to advance the discussion of antisemitism on university campuses, it must be recognized that Jews are a minority group that are still in need of understanding and compassion. Unfortunately, for many Jewish scholars:

> After centuries of experiencing other people not coming to our defense when we were targeted by violence and persecution, Jews have internalized the idea that there's no hope of getting other people to stand with us. For Jews who struggle for social justice, that means we often stay quiet about anti-Jewish oppression: We learn to fight in support of other groups without requesting the solidarity we, ourselves, need. (Rosenblum, 2007, p. 9)

Therefore, it is vital that all multiculturalists begin to stand up and address antisemitism in their university courses; simply, Jews are just too few in number to fight this battle alone.

ACKNOWLEDGMENT

An earlier version of this chapter appeared as: Rubin, D. I. (2018). The muddy waters of multicultural acceptance: A qualitative case study on antisemitism and the Israeli/Palestinian conflict. *Journal of Ethnic and Cultural Studies*, *5*(1), 1–15. Used here and modified with permission from the publishers.

NOTE

[1] This refers to the predominance of Ashkenazi Jews in the U.S., not the Sephardim and Mizrahim.

CHAPTER 8

JEWISH ACADEMICS' EXPERIENCES OF ANTISEMITISM WITHIN THE UNITED STATES

INTRODUCTION

As discussed throughout this text, racism against Jews, in the form of antisemitism, is still quite prevalent in the United States today. According to Astor (2018), antisemitic incidents were reported across all 50 states for the first time in at least a decade. This is cause for great concern for Jews across the U.S. Pallade (2009) has asserted that, "Anti-Semitism in academia is by no means a new phenomenon, nor is it an unusual one" (p. 34). Unfortunately, antisemitism is felt by both faculty and students alike in the form of harassment, vandalism, and assault (Astor, 2018). In order to address the issue of antisemitism in the university workplace, this study attempted to ascertain whether Jewish university and college professors have experienced prejudice and discrimination for being Jewish, in both their personal and professional lives. To understand Jewish professors' thoughts and feelings about perceived antisemitism, a mixed-method research study was conducted to give voice to those who believe they have been victims of anti-Jewish sentiment at some point in their lives. This study identified professors' experiences with anti-Jewish attitudes, and it also shed a light on the harmful treatment that some have received on their university campuses simply for identifying as Jewish.

PERCEPTION OF ANTISEMITISM

There are many different definitions of antisemitism in academic literature, and for the purpose of this study, it is defined as "prejudice, hostility, and discrimination toward Jews as a religious or cultural group that can manifest on an individual, institutional, or societal level" (Schlosser et al., 2007, p. 118). This study does not focus on the rationale for the perception of being discriminated against; it takes one's beliefs at face value. Therefore, in this study, "A paramount determinant of the perception of anti-Semitism is the individual's belief that he or she has experienced it" (Rebhun, 2014, p. 44).

Therefore, if a participant believes that s/he was discriminated against and treated negatively solely due to being Jewish, then it is believed to be an act of antisemitism.

Rebhun (2014) has asserted that, "As a major religio-ethnic group in the United States, Jews are exposed to the possibility of experiences and self-perceptions of anti-Semitism. Anti-Semitism views Jews as a collective or personal threat in various respects – social, economic, political, and so on" (p. 44). People can be victims of antisemitism in a myriad of ways – everything from nonverbal interactions, such as hostile facial expressions, to more demonstrable activities, such as rallies and violent crimes (Chanes, 1999; Tobin, 1988). While it has believed that many factors, such as one's age, gender, geographic location, education, and group identity, may influences one's perception of antisemitism (F. Cohen, 2010; Rebhun, 2014), acts of antisemitism continue to rise. Data from a recent study by the Center for the Study of Hate and Extremism shows that, "Jews are consistently the most targeted religious group, and [they] represented 19 percent of all hate crimes reported in major cities in 2017" (Hauslohner, 2018, p. 1). The unfortunate reality is that many hate crimes go unreported in the U.S. every year (Yadidi, 2017), so the actual number of antisemitic acts committed against Jews is simply impossible to know with certainty.

HOSTILITY ON U.S. CAMPUSES

It has been found that there has been a significant increase in antisemitic acts on U.S. college and university campuses in the past several years (Farber & Poleg, 2019; Ward & Levin, 2019). The Report on Antisemitic Activity at U.S. Colleges and Universities (2015) noted that campus antisemitism is still quite prevalent and that there is a strong correlation between the number and presence of anti-Zionist groups on campus (and faculty supporting the Boycott, Divest, and Sanctions [BDS] movement) and the amount of antisemitic activity on college campuses (Amcha Initiative, 2015). Harris and Shichtman (2018) asserted that, "BDS has also created a path from anti-Israeli to antisemitic behavior among university students" (p. 163). According to a study that focuses on the University of California (UC) campuses, Beckwith (2011) found that antisemitic speech and activity has occurred for more than a decade on UC campuses, and they are often initiated by the pro-Palestinian and Muslim student groups as well as by academic faculty. It is unfortunate that many Jewish scholars have been victim to racism and discrimination in their lives and that many have had to confront intolerance from their own students and colleagues. Unfortunately, research studies seldomly address religious discrimination in the workplace. It has been found that religious claims filed with the Equal Employment Opportunity Commission (EEOC) have more than doubled in the last 20 years (Cantone & Weiner, 2017).

In this research study, participants were asked to explain any *beliefs* or *feelings* of negative treatment due to their being Jewish. While there might be a difference between perceptions of antisemitism (even recall of incidents) and actual racist incidents, it is impossible to truly separate the two. While it is still important to "question the reliability of survey reports of being a victim" (J. E. Cohen, 2010, p. 93), perception is vital to gauge victimization of antisemitism.

METHODOLOGY

This mixed-methods study was conducted via survey. In order to obtain data about U.S. college/university professors' perceptions of antisemitism (n = 93), I created a ten-question online survey using SurveyMonkey©. After receiving IRB approval in late January 2018 from Jacksonville State University (Alabama, U.S.), I posted the multiple-choice survey, with accompanying space for participants to add further detail and explanation to their responses. I searched for Jewish study participants who were college or university faculty in the U.S. holding all academic ranks (i.e., from adjunct to professor Emerita). In order to solicit faculty participation, I initially invited, via email, 16 Jewish university faculty members to participate in the survey; I had personal knowledge of these academics due to my study on antisemitism and the Israeli/Palestinian conflict (see the previous chapter). I requested that the invited study participants forward my email invitation to any Jewish scholars in the U.S. they may be familiar; this process is known as snowball sampling (Johnson & Christensen, 2012).

In addition to contacting the initial academic faculty, I emailed two groups that cater to Jewish academics: the Academic Engagement Network (AEN) and Scholars for Peace in the Middle East (SPME). I emailed the directors my initial participation email and requested that they invite their members to participate. I also researched large synagogues in the U.S. via Google and found an article about "America's 25 Most Vibrant Congregations" (Newsweek, 2009). After some online research, I emailed all of the congregations' media directors and requested that my study be shared with their members. I only received a response from three of the congregations, with two accepting and one declining to participate. Lastly, I performed a Google search of Jewish Studies and Judaic Studies university programs in the U.S. I proceeded to "cold email" the department heads and/or program directors of 182 programs, requesting their participation in the study and to forward my email to their department members and any of their Jewish colleagues in all academic departments.

Due to the nature of this sensitive research study, all participant identities remain anonymous; there was no identifying information collected in the data collection, such as participants' names and particular academic institutions. The survey was officially closed in August 2018.

To analyze the written responses provided in the feedback portions of the survey, I used a critical discourse analysis (CDA) (Fairclough, 2001, 2005; McGregor, 2003). In brief, CDA is the investigation and analysis of how language is used (Barton, 2002; Hodges et al., 2008). This type of analysis is such a valuable tool in research studies because it helps explain the various power dynamics of social interactions. CDA addresses subjects such as social inequality, power, racism, and domination (Huckin et al., 2012; McGregor, 2003; Van Dijk, 1993). In particular, CDA is focused on the issues of control and power and the resulting injustice and inequity (Van Dijk, 1993). During the data analysis, several recurring themes emerged (McClaskey, 2008), and I coded the themes into specific categories for each question for analysis.

RESEARCH QUESTIONS

The research questions for this study are as follows:
1. Have you ever, in your lifetime, experienced verbal or physical harassment, discrimination, or intimidation of any kind for being Jewish?
2. Have you ever experienced verbal or physical harassment, discrimination, or intimidation of any kind for being Jewish while working at a college/university?

PARTICIPANT INFORMATION

For this study, there were a total of 93 participants, all of whom were employed by either two-year schools (n = 2) or four-year colleges or universities (n = 90) (one did not disclose her/his information). Full Professors were the largest group of study participants at 40.9% (n = 38); Adjunct Faculty and Professor Emerita were the smallest groups at 2.2% (n = 2 respectively). Respondents were almost equally divided by gender (female, n = 46; male, n = 45; two chose not to respond). The largest group of participants were 50–59 years old (n = 25); the smallest group were 20–29 years of age (n = 3). The Jewish study participants' religious and/or cultural affiliations varied. Reform Jews consisted of 25.8%

(n = 24); Conservative, 29% (n = 27); Orthodox, 9.7% (n = 9)[1]; and Secular (i.e., nonreligious), 22.6% (n = 21). Twelve participants preferred not to disclose their affiliation or identified as a different category (e.g., Reconstructionist).

PERSONAL EXPERIENCES WITH HARASSMENT

For the first research question in this study, I asked the participants: "Have you ever, in your lifetime, experienced verbal or physical harassment, discrimination, or intimidation of any kind for being Jewish?" Overwhelmingly, participants responded to the affirmative. In total, 68.8% (n = 64) said "Yes," while 31.2% (n = 29) said "No." There were several common themes that emerged from the research data: being the recipient of name-calling/insults/slurs, physical harassment/intimidation, online harassment, and physical/emotional isolation.

Verbal Harassment

According to Moulin (2016), "Evidence shows that adolescent Jews can be the victims of anti-Semitic prejudice at the hands of their school peers" (p. 686). This was certainly true for several of the participants in this study. Some commented about how they were verbally and physically harassed in their youth – ranging from elementary school through high school. One of the most prevalent forms of insult was hearing the pejorative use of the term "Jew." The Jewish academics documented being called derogatory terms such as "dirty Jew" and "fucking Jews." On one occasion, a respondent said that s/he was, "Buying a pizza, and it cost $20.01. I said I had a twenty with me, had a penny in the car, and would go get it. He responded, 'What do you think I am, a Jew?'" Several also recalled being called a "kike" and even a "kike dyke," just to name a few of the verbal insults mentioned in the data. Some of the study participants were called these names right to their faces while others were muttered under their breaths in close vicinity to them.

No matter the term, several study participants mentioned that they have been called so many racist names over the years, that is difficult to remember them all. As one study participant explained:

> It would be hard to describe all of it…I've been called a kike, asked why we killed Jesus. I've been warned not to tell my new boss that I'm not a Christian. The stuff you'd expect most Jews have experienced at some point or another.

CHAPTER 8

Several other participants noted that there was not enough space in the survey to document all of the times they have been victims of harassment. This was evident when one participant stated that s/he had been subject to abuse "More times than I can count." As another study participant observed:

> I grew up in Southern Indiana where there was widespread ignorance about Jews and Judaism, even within my own family (my father wasn't Jewish). It would be hard to isolate particular antisemitic comments from my years there, because they were so frequent.

It is important to remember that, unlike the "sticks and stones" song, words do matter, and they can cause a great deal of damage (Lasson, 2010). Psychological studies show that internalizing antisemitic beliefs can produce feelings of self-hatred, and this can result in feelings of embarrassment, anger, shame, and inferiority (Schlosser & Rosen, 2008).

Data from this study also showed that verbal harassment for being Jewish also took the form of the common trope of being cheap, shrewd, or miserly (Freedman, 2005; Gilman, 2003). Several study participants mentioned how they had heard the phrase – being "Jewed" or "Jewed down" (meaning that a person asserted that they were ripped off or haggled down in price somehow) in one situation or another. One participant explained how, "Once, on a vacation to Key West, a restaurant server who presumably did not know we were Jewish, talked about having been 'Jewed' down. Ugh...." As a Jewish academic living and teaching in the U.S., I also have had personal experience hearing the term "Jewed down," and it was in a doctoral-level social justice class, no less (see Chapter 2).

Several study participants mentioned that they had been victim to other forms of microaggressions, yet they did not provide any further detail or explanation. They did, interestingly, refer to these experiences as "the usual sort" or "typical stuff" – being victim to insults, "jokes," and other offensive situations that one just grins and bears. As stated by one participant, "I am sure that I have heard other off-handed remarks, but I think that I have taught myself to disassociate from them."

Study participants also commented on receiving racist literature (e.g., Neo-Nazi flyers) at their homes and universities. Others reported seeing antisemitic graffiti, such as swastikas, scratched into classroom furniture and hallway lockers, for example. One respondent stated that, "I've also come across hate speech (kike, swastikas) on the hallways in K-12 schools and universities where I have worked, in parks near my house, and carved into the desk in a room where I taught." Based upon the data obtained in this study, it is quite apparent that seeing antisemitic signs/symbols is certainly not an isolated incident for Jewish academics in the U.S.

Physical and Online Harassment

Jews can be identified as being Jewish in several ways, such as self-identification, "looking" Jewish, and wearing religious identifiers. According to Ghumman and Jackson (2008), "Religious identifiers are symbols or attire that religious group members don for religious purposes and that reveal their religious identity" (p. 240). For Jewish people, this can be in the form of wearing a yarmulke or a Star of David necklace, for example. Wearing Jewish identifiers can lead to instances of antisemitism.

Some study participants mentioned how they have been physically harassed or bullied for being Jewish. One of the most disturbing experiences that emerged from the data was when three participants had pennies thrown at them in school during childhood. According to one Jewish academic, "In junior high, kids threw pennies at the Jewish kids. I can't remember other details, but it wasn't a comfortable atmosphere." For some participants, physical harassment took on other forms. One respondent told how:

> When I was in junior high school and commuting via public transportation from my home in [New Jersey] to my Jewish school in [New York City], wearing a kippah [yarmulke], I was confronted by a group of teenagers who called me some anti-Semitic epithets. One spat on me.

Another study participant recalled how, when taking a bus, his yarmulke was grabbed off of his head. It is important to note that the participant said that after he had his yarmulke yanked off of his head, he calmly requested it be returned, and it was without further incident.

Some study participants also mentioned how they were made to feel foreign due to their "Jewish" looks. White Jews are often stereotyped as having curly hair, large noses, and dark eyes (Glenn, 2010; Schrank, 2007; Segal, 1999), and that can lead to being singled out for looking different somehow. As one respondent explained, "My first academic position was in the very deep south. Strangers would walk up behind me, stroke my hair, and say, 'Your hair is different!' (multiple times, typically at the Farmers' Market, Target, or other public spaces)." It is unclear whether or not those people knew that the respondent was Jewish, but she was definitely perceived as being foreign, the Other.

In the twenty-first century, antisemitic harassment now occurs online and on social media. One respondent stated that she no longer uses social media due to online harassment regarding the Holocaust. Another Jewish academic revealed that s/he "somehow ended up on a list called 'Shitlers List' online." A study participant also mentioned how he "gave a public lecture at a synagogue, which was recorded and put on YouTube. A number of the comments were virulently antisemitic." Harassment and bullying can take many forms and antisemitism continues to flourish online, such as on Twitter (Kunzelman, 2018).

Social Isolation

The last theme of social isolation also emerged from the study data. One scholar mentioned Christian privilege (Fairchild, 2009; Schlosser, 2003; Schlosser et al., 2009) as being a great concern, and as one study participant explained, there are "assumptions made in public contexts that everyone is Christian, or that everyone believes in God – that make me feel alienated from a community or an institution." Non-Jews are often uninformed about Jewish holidays, and several participants mentioned their grades suffering due to missing school days on High Holy days (i.e., Yom Kippur and Rosh Hashanah), even if they had notes from their parents to excuse them from missing classes. Jewish holidays were not just an issue for Jewish academics as students. One respondent even stated that, "As a middle school teacher long ago, my principal told me that my observance of Jewish holidays was 'an imposition on the rest of the staff.'"

Study participants explained how they were made to feel the Other in social situations because they were Jewish. One example was when a respondent explained how, "after college…someone at a wedding told me he 'could recognize the male Jews by their braids, but hadn't ever spoken to a female Jew before,' as if I was an exotic exhibit at a zoo." As mentioned earlier, I have also experienced this type of microaggression. On the first night of teaching a new course in diversity and multiculturalism at Jacksonville State University in the deep South, I mentioned my Jewish religious background, and a student told me proudly that meeting a Jewish person was on her "bucket list." As might be expected, even after some discussion in class, the student saw nothing inappropriate or offensive about her statement.

PROFESSIONAL EXPERIENCES OF HARASSMENT

For the second research question in this study, I asked the participants: "Have you ever experienced verbal or physical harassment, discrimination, or intimidation of any kind for being Jewish while working at a college/university?" More than a third of the respondents (39.1%) responded "Yes" (n = 36) while 59.8% said "No" (n = 55). One participant preferred not to respond. Four major themes emerged from the data: scheduling conflicts, hate speech, to be silent or silenced, and glass ceilings.

Jewish Holiday Scheduling Conflicts

At least six of the study participants mentioned scheduling of campus and department events/meetings on either Jewish High Holidays or on Shabbat (i.e., Friday at sundown until Saturday at sundown). It has been documented in previous research that Jewish educators "knew that their colleagues perceived differences *and drew attention to them*, as they did when they were absent from school for observances of the festivals or when they left school early on Friday in order to observe the Sabbath" (Haynes, 2003, p. 59). This is a difficult situation for many Jewish academics – they have to decide whether it is more important to observe their faith or attend a work meeting or class lecture. As one respondent claimed:

> There are other practices that go along with the discursive ones: sometimes ordering food for department functions that I can't eat (shellfish and pork), needing to clarify such matters, colleagues sending non-urgent department business e-mails but wanting a reply during the start of Shabbat, etc.

Many people are unable and/or unwilling to acknowledge their Christian privilege (Blumenfeld & Jaekel, 2012), and for many Jewish university faculty members, it seems that Jewish holidays are simply unimportant to their colleagues and administration. This puts many Jewish academics in an uncomfortable situation, one which creates tension and conflict with "colleagues when attempting to take time off or reschedule meetings due to holidays, etc." One participant stated that upon his tenure at a university, he asked a Jewish colleague what he did about the High Holy days. "No problem," he said. "You just call in sick. I pointed out that I wasn't sick; I was Jewish."

Verbal Harassment and Attacks

As discussed previously, several study participants mentioned how they have been exposed to antisemitic signs or symbols on their university campuses. Respondents mentioned how they had seen swastikas across campus, such as carved into bathroom stalls and classroom desks, spray painted on dormitory doors, and drawn on hallway walls.

Many study participants commented on their experiences hearing antisemitic comments, supposed "jokes," and inappropriate and attacking student comments in class. Jewish academics stated that they had heard comments about all Jews being rich, that they run the U.S., control the media, and even have "connections to accountants [and] film/TV producers." As mentioned by one study participant, "I have on more than one occasion had to correct a student who offered that Jews run the country, and especially the media establishment." From the data, it is apparent that Jewish stereotypes are alive and well on U.S. college campuses today.

Three participants detailed how they were verbally attacked during class due to the belief that Jews killed Jesus Christ. One professor was accused by a student of "killing her God" while other participants mentioned how they were told by students that they were going to hell because they were Jewish. Another study participant "was once screamed at during class by a student who went of a full-blown tirade about Jews killing Jesus and looking like monsters." In a similar vein, a Jewish professor described her uncomfortable experience with a student accusing Jews of being monsters and having horns. She explained that:

> after looking at a medieval image of Cain with horns, a conversation ensued about how contemporary Jews also have horns. When I prodded those students, they insisted that this was true about Jews – now and then. This class didn't realize that I was Jewish. I then told them that I was and lowered my head and said, 'Mine are retractable.' I tried to add some lightness and also reality to the conversation. I failed. Silence ensued.

The notion of Jews having horns and being connected with the Devil has existed for millennia (Bertman, 2009) and continues to this day.

The Need to Be Silent or Be Silenced

The next theme that emerged from the data is the need to conform in order to be accepted in the university culture. Some study participants noted that they were expected to either be silent or they felt that they were silenced by their colleagues. It has been found that, "Some American Jews will not openly identify as Jews unless they perceive the environment to be safe. This is because identifying oneself as Jewish can be perceived as potentially hazardous due to the long history of antisemitism" (Schlosser & Rosen, 2008,

p. 982). This is true, especially if a superior is considered to be antisemitic in some way. In other words, a Jewish scholar may be forced to keep her/his Jewish beliefs secret for fear that administration will act negatively and jeopardize the professor's academic career. An example of keeping silent was when one study participant stated that, "I was warned not to tell my new boss that I'm not Christian. When I asked why, the high-ranking colleague just told me that it would be bad for me and to just pretend." This sentiment was echoed several times in the conducted research – the fear of what would happen if s/he came out as Jewish to superiors.

Another concern for study participants was that they felt that they were being silenced for their religious beliefs. One respondent asserted that:

> the most common form [of negative treatment] I have experienced is absolute silence and being silenced. I have been excluded from university-wide policy committees on anti-Semitism. Furthermore, because I was not raised Jewish, colleagues seem to believe they can berate Jews and Jewish ideas in front of me with no recourse.

Several study participants also mentioned that they were told that they were "too Jewish" (whatever that means) and that were already "enough Jews in the department." This is another situation where Jewish academics may decide to keep their identities hidden, or muted at least, in order to get by in their departments.

At Catholic institutions in the U.S., a few commented that they have had wonderful experiences and that most students and faculty were respectful and asked many questions out of curiosity and the desire for understanding. There are, of course, those Jewish academics who have had less-than-positive experiences at Catholic institutions. As explained by one study participant:

> My other colleagues have no real sense of what it is like to be a Jew at a Catholic Institution and are totally uninterested. When I complain of discrimination or more subtle forms of antisemitism, they deny that it's taking place. Goodness knows why. I sometimes struggle with students…[b]ut mostly my discomfort comes from my colleagues. Mostly, I feel silenced. The problem is that my institution purports to care deeply about discrimination and othering, but I often feel that unless I conform, I have no 'place at the table.' Recently, I was asked by a committee that reviews course proposals what made the course (Philosophy of Literature) uniquely Catholic. I explained that it wasn't uniquely Catholic. I pointed out that my proposal explains how it contributes to

the Catholic mission of the university, but that I do not want to say to you or my students that there is something uniquely Catholic about it. For 45 minutes, I was asked repeatedly to say that it was Catholic. My response was always the same – this course was developed out of my experiences, out of my passions. I do not appreciate you silencing me. It was approved. But certain members of the committee refused to vote on it.

For this study participant, she came into conflict with her colleagues and felt silenced in the process. Her peers had no idea how difficult it was for a Jewish academic at a Catholic institution, and she felt excluded.

I would like to mention here that I have also had uncomfortable interactions at Catholic institutions. While attending a spring 2018 campus interview for a tenure-track faculty position at a private Roman Catholic research university in the Midwest, I felt out of place and even personally slighted. Just before eating lunch with the interview committee, the head of the committee stated that she wanted to say a prayer. I had no idea that it was going to be such a religious Christian blessing (evoking the name of Jesus). I felt incredibly uncomfortable, yet I stayed quiet because I did not want to ruin my chance at a job offer. Later that afternoon, I discreetly asked one of the interview committee members if saying prayers like that was customary at the institution. He responded that the prayer bothered him (as well) and that it had never occurred at any such luncheon he had attended during his years at the college.

The Glass Ceiling

The last theme to emerge from the data is the idea of there being a Jewish "glass ceiling;" that is, that some Jewish academics believed that they had difficulty advancing in their academic careers due to their religious affiliation. One study participant asserted that s/he had some suspicion of being denied tenure at a small liberal arts college because of being Jewish, but s/he had no direct evidence to support the belief. It was just a "gut feeling" (my choice of terms). Some respondents felt that they were held to different standards than their colleagues. For example, a study participant stated that, "the antisemitic chair of my department tried to keep me from getting tenure because I didn't meet standards higher than anyone else had to meet." Unfortunately, in instances such as these, there is often little concrete evidence to back up such assertions of antisemitism. If I, as the researcher, were able to follow up with the individual study participants, I might have been able to gather further evidence of antisemitism. Either way, it is still important for these stories to be shared and heard.

While some antisemitic acts were committed behind closed doors, some were done right out in the open. For example, one academic mentioned that when s/he was a candidate for a Dean's position at her university, s/he was told that the institution "would never hire a Jewish dean." Another academic stated that, "During my tenure process, I was harassed by my own department head who lied to the Dean of the college about my achievements." Now, it is unclear how the academic's Jewish background came into play here, but the participant must have felt that antisemitism was behind the behavior to warrant discussion in the study. The data show that feelings of antisemitism had a negative influence on several academics' careers. This is evident when one study participant shared her/his worst-case scenario. S/he asserted that, "Anti-Semitism caused me to resign my tenure at my previous institution, resulting in a federal investigation of my school. I am now leading a fight against campus anti-Semitism at my current university." Ultimately, the study data show that there is antisemitism in higher education, and this prevents some Jewish academics from reaching their full potential in their colleges and universities.

DISCUSSION

In her research of Jewish refugee academics in the early/mid twentieth century, Leff (2019) found that many colleges and universities in the U.S have a history of discrimination against Jewish academics (e.g., Harvard). It has also been noted that many universities refused to hire Jewish academics, and specific academic departments often had informal "one-Jew rule[s]" in their hiring practices (Leff, 2019, p. 105). Freidenreich (2007) stated that, "In the twenty-first century, Jews are extremely prominent and visible in academic circles, especially at prestigious universities in the United States" (p. 68). While this may be true in certain situations, Jewish academics only comprise 5% of American college and university professors (Gross & Simmons, 2009, p. 119). Jews are 2% of the U.S. population, which is only 3% less than their percentage in academia. This study shows that, in that small percentage of Jewish academics, there are some who feel that they have been discriminated against and treated in a hostile manner, in their personal and/or professional lives, simply for being Jewish.

The research data in this mixed-methods survey reveal some concerning trends. The majority of the Jewish study participants stated that they have

CHAPTER 8

been victims of antisemitic harassment in their personal lives (69%), and a large number have also felt some form(s) of antisemitism on their college and university campuses (39%). Tanenbaum (2013) found that more than a third of U.S. workers observed a religious bias in the workplace, and this study supports those findings. More than a third of the participants in this study claim to have experienced verbal or physical harassment, discrimination, or intimidation for being Jewish while working at a college/university.

In their personal lives, Jewish academics described being the recipient of antisemitic name-calling, physical harassment and/or intimidation, harassment on social media, and feeling physical and emotional isolation. In their professional lives, the study participants discussed problems with scheduling conflicts on important Jewish holidays, being the recipients of hate speech from both colleagues and students, having the feeling that they were expected to be silent or felt silenced institutionally, and that there were glass ceilings that they had difficulty breaking in order to be successful. Unfortunately, there has been little research on the pervasiveness of religious discrimination in the American workplace (Cantone & Weiner, 2017; Ghumman et al., 2013; Scheitle & Ecklund, 2018), especially as they pertain to college and university employment. These issues of discrimination and hostility are concerning and warrant further study and analysis.

CONCLUSION

Antisemitism has been growing significantly on college and university campuses across the U.S. in recent years. Unfortunately, there are few, if any, studies that address issues of antisemitism with Jewish academics at the university level. In the survey discussed in this chapter, many study participants described their experiences with intolerance and bigotry across the timeline – from youth to the present day. In academia, this can range from work requirements on Jewish High Holidays, being verbally attacked by students for killing Jesus Christ, and being held personally responsible for the treatment of Palestinians in the Middle East. Due to microaggressions and larger acts of antisemitism in the U.S., many Jewish academics feel uncomfortable identifying as Jewish, both at work and in their everyday routines. Antisemitism is not isolated to one area of Jewish lives; discrimination and bigotry extends and connects all aspects of their existence. Therefore, this research study supports the assertion that "many American Jews will have a personal experience with antisemitism at some point in their lives; nearly all Jews are impacted by acts of antisemitism vicariously" (Schlosser, 2006, p. 433).

FUTURE RESEARCH

Schlosser (2003) noted that, "the ways in which I am privileged have also led to the neglect and denial of the part of me that experiences oppression" (p. 46). In a study by MacDonald-Dennis (2006), he found that many of his Jewish study participants minimized the impact of antisemitism on their lives. In this study, several participants mentioned having personal experiences with antisemitism (e.g., being called derogatory names, having pennies thrown at them) and then immediately minimized and dismissed the acts by describing them as the "typical stuff" and "the usual sort" of things that happen to Jewish people today. Internalized antisemitism, or when Jews believe the negative stereotypes and messages that are believed to be true by those outside of the Jewish community (Rosenwasser, 2002), is also evident in the minimization of one's personal experiences of antisemitism. There is no name for this type of minimalization, and I believe it needs to be researched more thoroughly in the future.

LIMITATIONS

There are limitations to the findings in this study. The small sample size (n = 93) prevents generalizability across the larger U.S. Jewish population. In addition, with larger feedback space in the survey or opportunity to follow up with personal interviews, participants could have further elaborated on issues that might have been just mentioned in passing. With personal interviews, study participants could have also asked for clarification if they did not clearly understand the interview questions.

NOTE

[1] The groups are listed in order from most liberal to most conservative/traditional on the basis of their values and adherence to Jewish doctrine.

CHAPTER 9

THE STEREOTYPICAL PORTRAYAL OF JEWISH MASCULINITY ON *THE BIG BANG THEORY*

INTRODUCTION

The stereotypical image of the Jewish male has long been viewed as negative in U.S. society, and this less-than-flattering depiction has continued due to the advent of television. On the popular comedy, *The Big Bang Theory* (CBS, 2007–2019), Howard Joel Wolowitz, played by Simon Helberg, is an engineer at a prestigious university in southern California. Howard is also the epitome of the stereotypical Jewish male; he is thin, awkward, big-nosed, and a mamma's boy; basically, a *nebbish*. For much of the series, thirty-something-year-old Howard still lived at home with his mother until her passing during season eight (due to the death of Carol Ann Susi in 2014, the actress who portrayed her). This type of negative portrayal of the Jewish man is not uncommon in the United States (Grinberg, 2014). Even though the presence of Jewish characters on television in the United States, including leading roles, has increased since the 1980s (Rockler, 2006), they are still often portrayed stereotypically and negatively. According to Baskind (2007):

> Jews in American popular entertainment convey Otherness in one of three ways: by the discrimination they experienced, through flagrant stereotypes, or by concealing or merely implying their Jewishness. Since the advent of the motion picture and later television, there was little inherently positive about Jews in general pop culture. (p. 4)

While some Jews, like Jerry Seinfeld (*Seinfeld*, NBC, 1989–1998), are still widely known in popular culture, their Jewishness is almost, if not completely, hidden from the viewer. When Jewish television characters show their Jewishness, they are often depicted stereotypically.

Although seemingly harmless on the surface, the character of Howard Wolowitz is troublesome due to the messages he conveys to the viewer. Primarily, researchers have found that stereotypes on television may influence people's biases and perceptions (Ruggieri & Leebron, 2010), and this false

© DANIEL IAN RUBIN, 2021 | DOI:10.1163/9789004464087_009

representation of a Jewish man can affect both Jews and non-Jews alike. While many psychologists would agree that, "Jewish identity is a complex, multifaceted construct that is affected by numerous influences and is content-specific" (Schlosser et al., 2009, p. 54), negative stereotypes on television programs can affect how groups of people are perceived (Mastro et al., 2008; Punyanunt-Carter, 2008). This can then, in turn, affect the self-esteem of those being stereotyped (Martins & Harrison, 2012).

According to Gerson (2018), "biologically based definitions of Jewishness have no meaning without understanding the social and cultural forces that generate and sustain them" (p. 13). Therefore, this chapter will explore the depiction of Jewish male masculinity[1] in society and on television, in the United States. The inexorable link between the emasculated Jewish male and his mother will also be explored in relation to the Jewish male stereotype on prime-time television programming. In addition, the character of Howard Wolowitz will be discussed through a critical lens while addressing negative Jewish male representation and its potential concerns in a larger global context.

A BRIEF DEPICTION OF THE JEWISH MALE
(AND HIS MOTHER, OF COURSE)

For centuries, Jews around the world have been persecuted and discriminated against due to religious and socioeconomic reasons. In the eyes of many, Jews were seen as being dirty, deceitful, swarthy, ugly (i.e., having beady eyes and large noses), and even diseased (Benton, 2015; Gilman, 1994; Segal, 1999; Weinbaum, 1998). For Jewish men, believed to hold core values of social justice and peace (Schlosser, 2006), their masculinity had also been called into question. This resulted in being relegated to a "stereotype in fin-de-siecle European culture of Jewish men as feminized in both body and character" (Hyman, 2002, p. 156). In the United States, Jewish masculinity continued to be influenced by European beliefs. As such, Jewish males continued to be seen as weak, passive (i.e., unwilling to fight back), and effeminate, both physically and mentally (Grinberg, 2014; Norwood, 2009; Ravits, 2000). If that were not enough, Jewish men were also believed to be greedy, power-hungry (Berinsky & Mendelberg, 2005), and horrible at playing sports (Byers & Krieger, 2005).

In the late 1800s and early 1900s in the U.S., this negative perception began to change, at least in small doses. Due to the struggle for self-preservation, some inner-city Jewish males took up the art of fighting (boxing, in particular) due to the ever-present fear of beatings from Gentiles and anti-Semites in neighboring communities (Norwood, 2009). Many Jewish males "began to forge a new muscular identity" that helped to dispel some of the negative stereotypes of "Jewish males' physical incapacity, cowardice, and effeminacy that dated almost from the beginning of the Second Diaspora" (Norwood, 2009, p. 168). Many Jewish fighters, such as Max Baer, were quite popular in the sport in the early twentieth century and many others learned to protect themselves and their loved ones due to their newfound combative prowess; unfortunately, the notion of the hyper-masculine Jew was not widely accepted on a large scale.

Jewish men were perceived by white Anglo-Saxon Protestant (WASP) society as coming from a culture that emphasized morality and literacy, which was seen as emasculating (Martel, 2001), yet the notion of the verbally combative intellectual Jew, especially in urban areas such as New York City, soon came to prominence (Grinberg, 2014). According to Freedman (2005), "In the 1950s, this model flipped around, as the de-masculinized – or at least *schlumpy* – Jewish intellectual became something of a cultural icon not despite but because of his difference from robust WASP norms of masculinity" (p. 91). Therefore, although still not respected for their physical and emotional strength, Jewish men gained a certain level of respect for their intellectual, studious nature. Ultimately, the Jewish males' "combination of intellectualism and physical deficiencies were the subject of much early twentieth-century worrying…culminating in, or at least continuing through, the films of Woody Allen and the novels of Philip Roth" (Freedman, 2005, p. 90). Even though the process of Zionism ushered in a new era of perceived Jewish toughness (Martel, 2001), this did not really affect the stereotypical representation of Jewish males in the U.S. media.

The modern stereotypical image of the Jewish male is aligned predominantly with awkward and meek characters portrayed by the likes of Woody Allen rather than that of masculine Jewish athletes, such as Sandy Koufax (professional U.S. baseball player for the Brooklyn/Los Angeles Dodgers) and Julian Edelman (of the New England Patriots NFL team). There are rarely, if ever, depictions of Jewish males on popular television that display a personality and physical characteristics that stray far from the previously described stereotype. One exception is Bill Goldberg, a 6'4, 285-pound, (semi-retired) professional wrestler in World Wrestling Entertainment (WWE). He is an incredibly popular wrestler who fights under his real name (i.e., referred to as "Goldberg"); his legion of fans even chant his name during his entrance to the ring. Goldberg is nothing but pure strength and aggression. Although

CHAPTER 9

it was believed by Benton (2015) that Goldberg "made his Jewishness a central feature of his character without utilizing defined stereotypes" (p. 409), the only thing that really identifies Goldberg as being Jewish is his name; he never identifies as Jewish in the ring by wearing any regalia displaying Jewish symbols. Out of the ring, he has declared his Jewishness, but it was a rare occurrence. For example, on the back-jacket cover of his autobiography, he is seen wearing a yarmulke (Goldberg & Goldberg, 2000). Goldberg even said that, "I figured the name Goldberg said it all. Hell, if I walk out there as Goldberg and you can't figure out I'm Jewish for yourself, well, then, I'm sorry" (Spalding, 2000, p. 2). Therefore, although Goldberg helps to break the stereotype of the weak, intellectual, office-working Jew, he could be considered to be an "inferred" or "crypto" Jew (Byers & Krieger, 2005). Byers and Krieger (2005) said that crypto and inferred Jews "are often constructed as non-Jewish on the narrative's surface but are imbued with Jewishness through subtext or via various coded signifiers. These make up an increasing proportion of the 'Jewish' characters to be studied" (p. 134). Goldberg is only really recognizable as Jewish due to his name, and if some do not know that Goldberg is a Jewish surname, his religious background can be, and likely is, missed.

THE JEWISH MOTHER

According to television stereotypes, no good Jewish boy can be discussed without his mother, and the first Jewish mother depicted on U.S. radio, and then television, was in the form of Molly Goldberg. *The Goldbergs* (CBS, NBC, & DuMont, 1949–1954), which told the story of a first-generation immigrant family from Europe, is considered to be the first successful television sitcom (Brook, 1999a). The show focused on "the trials and tribulations of a poor Jewish family who are guided through their difficult times by a warm, compassionate, and understanding woman, Molly Goldberg played by Gertrude Berg" (Cantor, 1991, p. 208). The (fake) Yiddish-accented Molly was portrayed as an overweight, doting, nurturing, warm, and generous working-class Jewish matriarch (Brook, 1999b; Ruggieri & Leebron, 2010). While a beloved television character, "[Berg's] early portrayal of the Jewish female became synonymous with the stereotyped overweight, well-meaning, but overbearing mother" (Ruggieri & Leebron, 2010, p. 1272).

The stereotype of the Jewish mother was made popular in the United States by male comedy writers during the 1960s[2] (Ravits, 2000). Ultimately, Jewish mothers were portrayed as nagging, nitpicky, overprotective, manipulative, overbearing, domineering, pushy, guilting, and loving to an extreme (Baskind, 2007; Clanton, 2013; Ravits, 2000; Rockler, 2006). The Jewish mother loved too much and knew absolutely no boundaries in order to protect her sons. Howards' mother on *The Big Bang Theory* is never seen but always heard (literally and metaphorically). Mrs. Wolowitz was described consistently as being obese and immensely overbearing; therefore, she exuded most of the negative stereotypes of the Jewish mother described earlier.

THE TELEVISION DEPICTION OF THE JEWISH MALE

According to Buchbinder (2008), "The representation of inadequate masculinities, and particularly of the male-as-schlemiel [inadequately or incompetently male], is hardly a new development in either film or television" (p. 232); this has been occurring for decades and continues to this day. Characters such as the neurotic Miles Silverberg on *Murphy Brown* (CBS, 1988–1998, 2018), whiny Joel Fleischman on *Northern Exposure* (CBS, 1990–1995), and prissy and obsessive Schmidt on *New Girl* (FOX, 2011–2018) are just the tip of the Jewish-character iceberg. While all of these characters are bright and successful in their white-collar careers, they all epitomize the negative stereotype of the weak Jewish male; they are more neurotic and whiny and less strong and outwardly masculine (e.g., in stature, attitude, career) than many other non-Jewish male characters on modern-day television.

It should be noted that comedic character portrayals on television sitcoms are often depicted stereotypically, also referred to as "stock types" (Ravits, 2000). Byers and Krieger (2005) concurred that, "It is true that, on television, difference often enters the text through the stereotype because the stereotype allows viewers to 'read' a character very quickly, in a 'short hand'" (p. 132); therefore, stereotypes are simply cognitive shortcuts (Valdivia, 2010). It is understood in this critique that most, if not all, television characters are stereotyped to a certain degree. While addressing Jewish masculinity on popular television, "it is not stereotypes per say that are objectionable but the constant deployment of stereotypes that serve to demean and discriminate against segments of the population" (Valdivia, 2010, p. 170). The major issue to be addressed here is how the stereotypical representation of the emasculated male is detrimental to Jewish people and the perception of Jews as a whole.

As stated previously, the portrayal of the hapless, bumbling, Jewish geek can be seen in many television and movie roles in recent memory. Howard Wolowitz is just another in a long line of awkward, overly sensitive, meek Jewish men in television history. For example, most of Ben Stiller's film roles (both acted and voiced) are considered to be in this tradition, as well as David Schwimmer's role as Ross Gellar on the hit comedy *Friends* (NBC, 1994–2004) (Buchbinder, 2008), along with the character of Dr. John (J. D.) Dorian on the comedy *Scrubs* (NBC, 2001–08; ABC, 2009–2010). Their Jewishness is alluded to, perhaps inferred, but their Jewish beliefs are rarely if ever displayed. Howard may wear his Jewishness on his sleeve, but he is still portrayed negatively and stereotypically.

THE WOLOWITZ CONUNDRUM

The Big Bang Theory (CBS, 2007–2019) went off the air in spring 2019 as the No. 1 sitcom on U.S. television, and it held that position for most of the previous eight years (Fitzgerald, 2019). The show revolves around four brilliant and socially awkward university scientists: the "intellectually gifted theoretical physicist Sheldon Cooper, his roommate applied physicist Leonard Hofstadter, astrophysicist Rajesh Koothrappali, and engineer Howard Wolowitz" (McIntosh, 2014, pp. 195–196). Sheldon, Leonard, and Rajesh all hold PhDs, while Howard has a Master's degree from the Massachusetts Institute of Technology (MIT) in engineering; therefore, he often is mocked and ridiculed for not having a PhD like his peers. All four friends enjoy playing fantasy board games together, watching Star Trek and other sci-fi films, and hanging out at the local comic book shop. Howard is the only Jewish person out of the four Caltech scientists (Uliss, 2015). The additional female characters on the program – Penny (Hofstadter), Bernadette Rostenkowski, and Amy Farrah Fowler – are the love interests (then spouses) of Leonard, Howard, and Sheldon respectively. All of the women are portrayed as Christian, which is interesting to note since Amy Farrah Fowler, played by Mayim Bialik, and Bernadette Rostenkowski, played by Melissa Rauch, are actually Jewish in real life. Be that as it may, Howard is the only major Jewish character on the popular show.

Before even seeing the character of Howard Wolowitz on screen, the viewer is provided with subtle messages about Howard's character. First of all, the name Wolowitz is troublesome, for this surname, coincidental or not, has "wallow" in it, which reeks of the whiny, wimpy, Jewish male stereotype. People who wallow are not active doers; they are passive complainers. For those viewers knowledgeable of Jewish names, especially Ashkenazi-esque nomenclature, Wolowitz is a dead giveaway of Howard's Jewish background. When Howard is then seen on screen, one can understand how he portrays the ultimate Jewish male stereotype. Howard is a "physically small, even timid, man who is awkward around women, often exaggerating his masculinity and prowess, and who still lives with his overbearing mother" (Clanton, 2013, p. 1).

Howard demonstrates his lack of masculinity repeatedly throughout the series, so much so that it would take another article entirely to provide all of the examples to support this claim. Here are just a few choice bits: Howard can best be described as a creep, slimy even, in his early interactions with women. During Season Two, in an episode called "The Vegas Renormalization," Howard has intercourse with a woman he meets on a road trip to Las Vegas. When Howard finds out that the woman is a prostitute and is just providing him with the "Jewish girlfriend experience" (with accompanying fake New York accent), he gleefully has sex with her anyway because his friends have already paid for her services.

During an episode in Season Three called "The Creepy Candy Coating Corollary," Howard had, "His first date with his future wife, Bernadette, [it] goes horribly until they start bonding over how overprotective their respective mothers are" (Clanton, 2013, p. 2). Therefore, Howard is unable to charm Bernadette with his own personality; it takes complaining about his mother for them both to find a common interest. Furthermore, in his relationship with Bernadette, Howard is still dominated by a woman. Although not as heavy-handed as Howard's mother, Debbie Wolowitz, Bernadette still controls Howard's actions. Creepily, Howard also feels that when Bernadette gets angry and yells, sounding just like his mother, Bernadette sounds sexy. Somehow, Howard does not make the connection between the similar vocal tonalities of his wife and of his own mother.

In Season Four's episode called "The Alien Parasite Hypothesis," Howard and his best friend, Raj, argue over which of them would be best suited as the superhero and which would be the sidekick; so, to in order to solve their dispute, they decide to wrestle for the title of lead hero. While circling each other on the wrestling mat, Howard brags about taking a karate lesson when he was eleven, yet he shows his innate fear and weakness when he never actually makes contact with Raj during the whole proceeding. He is all talk and no action.

In Season Six, during an episode titled "The Decoupling Fluctuation," Howard is harassed and bullied by his fellow astronauts while on a mission to the International Space Station. His fellow astronauts even nickname Howard "Fruit Loop" due to an overheard conversation between he and his mother regarding the breakfast cereal (Fruit Loops). Howard is too scared to confront the bullies, who call him names and even draw on his face while sleeping, so he complains instead to his wife and mother via Skype in his search for solace.

Lastly, in the Season Eight episode called "The Expedition Approximation," we find out that Howard has to earn stars on a "chore chart" created by his wife, Bernadette, in order to purchase desired items on eBay (e.g., *Star Trek* collectors' plates). Although it has been common knowledge for several seasons that Bernadette earns much more money than Howard in her pharmaceutical research position, we find out that he receives an allowance from his wife for completing his chores at home. Therefore, Howard falls prey to several other weak male stereotypes – not only does he make significantly less money than his wife, he is also treated like a child for not being a productive and strong spouse.

REPRESENTATION OF JUDAISM

In *The Big Bang Theory*, there are sporadic references to Judaism, such as Howard inviting (or rather, nagging) a date over for Shabbat dinner, Howard's Bar Mitzvah and the savings bonds that were given to him, as well as an occasional sprinkling of Yiddish (e.g., *putz* and *fakakta*). Mrs. Wolowitz's cooking, her "melt in your mouth" brisket, in particular, is also a topic that arises every now and again. Unfortunately:

> In spite of the increased presence of Jewish references and the knowledge of Judaism the series assumes on the part of the viewer as compared to previous television series, *The Big Bang Theory* doesn't depict Judaism as serving as a resource for action, identity, or meaning-making for Howard. (Clanton, 2013, p. 1)

Judaism and Jewish concepts are simply just a means to a punchline on the program, with many of the jokes coming at the expense of Howard's relationship with his mother. The loud, apparently obese woman is never actually seen on the show, yet her booming voice is heard throughout the house. According to Clanton (2013), Mrs. Wolowitz has a loud, "grating, nasal, New Jersey-esque, always screaming voice" (p. 2). Once again, Howard's mother epitomizes the negative Jewish mother stereotype, including the traditional, east coast, New York/New Jersey accent.

The series creator of *The Big Bang Theory*, Chuck Lorre, has said in interviews that, "Wolowitz is based on [my] own Jewish background as well as that of [Simon] Helberg" (Wills, 2009, p. 1). Lorre went on to say that,

'Things are loud in a Jewish household…That's just the way we talk…That was the fun of creating that off-camera mother. That's how communication happens in some households, and it's normal in that house" (Wills, 2009, p. 1). It is completely acceptable and understandable that Lorre would use his own personal background and experiences to create a television series. The issue is that when a program is created by a Jewish man, and the one Jewish protagonist on his program is portrayed stereotypically as both weak and a mama's boy, this is problematic.

All of the male characters on *The Big Bang Theory* are quirky and nerdy, yet none of the other characters of Sheldon, Leonard, or Raj fall into prescribed stereotypes based upon their race, ethnicity, or religion. While Sheldon is eccentric and appears to suffer from various neuroses and personality disorders (e.g., it has been debated whether he is on the autism spectrum) (Winston, 2016), he is not characterized by his religious/ethnic beliefs. Sheldon is an agnostic who was raised Evangelical Christian in the heart of Texas, and his character revolves around his eccentric behavior and lack of understanding of social interaction. Leonard's religious background is Christian, yet his character is not framed by his religious beliefs, which only really emerge during Christmastime anyway (i.e., in the form of a tree and presents). Raj, originally from India, is a self-professed Hindu, yet his character revolves around his social anxieties (in the earlier seasons) and his continued lackluster love-life. His religious beliefs arise occasionally (e.g., in his discussion of his love of hamburgers in "The Thanksgiving Decoupling," Season 7, Episode 9), yet his Hinduism plays no real part in his represented persona. The character of Howard Wolowitz breaks from the program's lack of focus on religious identity.

Wolowitz is different from the other characters in that he is simply seen as the stereotypical Jewish male. Although, Howard is talented at playing the piano, has been to the international space station, and knows Stephen Hawking (as shown in "The Hawking Excitation"), he is still the epitome of the weak Jewish male. His character revolves around his weakness and his subordination to women, and most, if not all, of his comedic scenarios are due to his meek character traits. For example, in the Season Four episode titled "The Robotic Manipulation," Howard borrows a robot from the Jet Propulsion Laboratory and must be rushed to the hospital because the machine "somehow" gets latched onto his male phallus. While Howard has a brilliant mind, his social ineptitude with women and overall *nebbish*-ness (i.e., his timid or submissive character) lead to his comedic flair. Due to the heavy focus on Howard's Jewishness, his character is seen as Jewish first and nerdy, dickey-wearing engineer second. This perpetuation of negative Jewish male (and female) stereotypes come at a cost, to both Jews and non-Jews alike.

TELEVISION, STEREOTYPES, AND PERCEPTION

According to Ruggieri and Leebron (2010), "television remains a primary source for entertainment for millions of Americans, whose opinions of women and ethnic groups are influenced by character portrayals on television" (p. 1266). For those people who watch television programming on a regular basis, stereotypical (i.e., often biased and unfavorable) portrayals of women and people of color have a significant influence on the viewing audience (Arendt & Northup, 2015; Martins & Harrison, 2012; Mastro et al., 2008; Mastro et al., 2009; Punyanunt-Carter, 2008). Television stereotypes may influence interpretations and biases against Jews in the real world (Ruggieri & Leebron, 2010).

It is important to note that the United States is not alone in its use of negative stereotypes on television programming. Tukachinsky et al. (2015) asserted that, "The tendency to negatively depict and underrepresent ethnic, national and religious minorities in media has been documented in many countries" (p. 34), such as the portrayal of Muslims in the United Kingdom and Arabs on Israeli television. That being said, there appears to be little to no available research that studies the influence of stereotypical Jewish television characters on both Jewish and non-Jewish viewers in the U.S. Therefore, it is important to review how negative stereotypes of people of color on television affect White television viewers as well as people of color themselves.

In research conducted by Mastro et al. (2008), it was found that when White people in the U.S. view even a minimal amount of negative portrayals of Latinxs on television programming, they perceive them more negatively. With regard to African American characters on television, Punyanunt-Carter (2008) theorized that negative portrayals of "African Americans on television may have an influence on viewers and their perceptions about African Americans in general" (p. 251). A study by Arendt and Northup (2015) found that regular, long-term exposure to negative stereotypes of specific racial groups on television news programs appeared to create negative "implicit attitudes" (i.e., involuntary gut responses) about those particular groups with the program viewers. In other words, how people of color are represented on television news and programming affects how viewers' social realities are constructed (referred to as "cultivation") (Ibrahim & Wolf, 2011). Research has shown a correlation between negative representation of particular racial and ethnic groups on television and negative perception of those groups (Arendt & Northup, 2015; Hurley et al., 2015; Mastro et al., 2009; Punyanunt-Carter, 2008).

While there are few studies pertaining to Jewish perception based on television programming, due to the research findings presented earlier, it is possible, if not probable, that viewing negative stereotypes of Jewish males on U.S. television programs influences viewer perception of Jewish men, and in the case of *The Big Bang Theory*, Jewish women (i.e., mothers), as well. The continued portrayal of both the wimpy Jewish male and the overbearing Jewish mother can send subtle (or not so subtle) messages that Jewish men are weak, whiny, and hypersensitive, while Jewish mothers are loud, obnoxious, and overly critical. It is important to note that, as mentioned previously, antisemitism is at record levels in the U.S. Recently, there is even a "global trend of anti-Semitic hate speech blaming Jews and Israelis for the coronavirus" (Estrin, 2020, para. 1). In addition, antisemitism is on the rise in both the United States and around the world (Reich, 2020; Roach, 2019), stereotypical Jewish representation on television programming is of great concern due to its potential influence on Jewish perception.

In addition, stereotypical and/or negative representations of particular groups on television affect one's sense of self. For example, repeated exposure to stereotypical portrayals of Native Americans, such as via sports mascots and characters in television and film (e.g., Disney's *Pocahontas*), has been found to have negative, harmful consequences to one's self and community worth (Davis-Delano et al., 2020; Fryberg et al., 2008). Research by Martins and Harrison (2012) found that exposure to television programming predicted a decrease in the self-esteem of all children except for White males. Therefore, it appears that when non-White children view racial stereotypes repeated on television, the children compare themselves to the images they see, which in turn, negatively affects their self-esteem (Martins & Harrison, 2012). It is possible to infer that viewing negative stereotypes of the emasculate, Jewish male on television programs have the power to not only negatively affect how non-Jews perceive Jewish people, but also, can harm the self-esteem of Jewish children. According to Ibrahim and Wolf (2011):

> As members of the Jewish community and non-Jewish people are exposed to television images that are reinforced through the ever-expanding newer electronic media, the cumulative effect of these messages is to more powerfully influence Jewish identity and the feelings of exclusion

from society expressed by these Jewish people. The result of this situation is that distorted media images create a situation whereby people who are unfairly represented struggle to find their own identity. (p. 305)

It is often believed that, "Some Jewish males absorb a kind of cultural low self-esteem: that we are weak and *nebbishy*" (Pfefferman, 2009, p. 1). This was definitely true for me growing up, despite living in a large city with a substantial Jewish population. It was not until the emergence of professional wrestling superstar, Bill Goldberg in the late 90s that I felt empowered by a masculine, Jewish male figure. Unfortunately, this was not until I was in my mid-twenties, which is rather late, in my opinion, to first see a strong Jewish role model. Due to the lack of strong Jewish male characters on U.S. television programming, it is possible that the perpetuation of the negative male image contributes to potential Jewish males' feelings of low self-esteem (i.e., internalized antisemitism).

CONCLUSION

Gerson (2018) posited that "we cannot conceptualize Jewish identity without gender. Jewishness is always gendered" (p. 13). Therefore, *The Big Bang Theory*, which was the most popular comedy on U.S. television for many years, is concerning and problematic for several reasons. Howard Wolowitz, the only Jewish central character on the show, is represented as the prototypical Jewish male; he is thin, gawky, weak, and domineered by women. Ravits (2000) asserted that, "The acceptance and popularity of Jewish humor in the entertainment industry – stand-up comedy, film, television, recordings, and literature – have contributed to the Jewish minority's increasing sense of security and success in the United States" (p. 29). While true to an extent, Jewish humor and the use of harmful stereotypes to convey that humor, does not come without a cost. A large body of research shows that stereotypes on television can negatively skew the perceptions and self-esteem of the viewer. Since Jews are such a small percentage of the U.S. population (2.1%) (Sheskin & Dashefsky, 2018), it is likely that many people believe the stereotypical depictions they see on *The Big Bang Theory* since they do not know any Jewish people in real life. Whether Jewish people in Hollywood are perpetuating a stereotypical view of Jewish life as in *The Big Bang Theory*, or others are doing it for them, the misrepresentation of Jewish men and women is harmful for both Jews and non-Jews alike.

IMPLICATIONS

It is not lost on me that "most situation comedies focus on superficial problems and are usually not created with the intent of contributing to political and cultural debates" (Rockler, 2006, p. 454). Television comedies never claim to address any real complex issues or concerns in society (e.g., the possible lack of people of color teaching at Howard's university, based on frequent scenes in the faculty cafeteria). If television comedies do approach any pertinent or contentious issues in society, they are usually surface level at best. Yet, in order to break the negative stereotype of the weak, Jewish male, which continues on popular television programs like *The Big Bang Theory* in the U.S., something needs to be done in the television industry. Although, according to Ravits (2000), "It is hard to fight oversimplification and stereotyping with more nuanced interpretations" (p. 20), television creators and writers need to take the lead to break the perpetuation of negative stereotypes aimed at Jewish people. If they do not, it is possible that the depiction of the Jewish male (and his mother) will continue to be seen negatively in U.S. society – now that is just *farkakte*.

ACKNOWLEDGMENT

An earlier version of this chapter appeared as: Rubin, D. I. (2021). The Stereotypical Portrayal of Jewish Masculinity on *The Big Bang Theory*. *The Journal of Popular Culture*, *54*(2). Used here and modified with permission from the publishers.

NOTES

[1] The definition of masculinity varies widely. For this chapter, masculinity will be defined as being strong, both physically and emotionally, confident, and competent.

[2] An example of the Jewish mother stereotype can be found in *Portnoy's Complaint* by Philip Roth (1969).

CHAPTER 10

CONCLUSION

Throughout time, Jews have held this precarious position in the world – hated at times; at others, accepted and held up as a "model minority" for other racial/ethnic groups to aspire to. Due to the perpetual existence of anti-Jewish animus, Antisemitism has been referred to as "history's oldest hatred" (Phillips, 2018, p. 1). The basis for this hatred runs deep. For example, according to Goldberg (2015):

> Europe has blamed the Jews for an encyclopedia of sins. The Church blamed the Jews for killing Jesus; Voltaire blamed the Jews for inventing Christianity. In the febrile minds of anti-Semites, Jews were usurers and well-poisoners and spreaders of disease. Jews were the creators of both communism and capitalism; they were clannish but also cosmopolitan; cowardly and warmongering; self-righteous moralists and defilers of culture. Ideologues and demagogues of many permutations have understood the Jews to be a singularly malevolent force standing between the world and its perfection. (pp. 4–5)

It is due to this never-ending hatred that Jews around the world have often hid their Jewish identities to avoid discrimination and persecution.

Soon after the death of six million Jews during the *Shoah*, at least in the United States, Jewish people started to become accepted in society for being White. They were tolerated as being Jewish as long as they were not seen as being too Jewish, great for television show punchlines and self-deprecating humor (see the previous chapter), but always to be seen with an ounce of distrust. Somehow, the notion that Jews were no longer an actual discriminated minority group became accepted, often internalized by Jews themselves. The game of comparative need always seemed to put Jews a far second to other groups calling for change.

As we progress through the twenty-first century, conspiracy movements, such as QAnon, continue to rehash antisemitic tropes that have existed for centuries (Wong, 2020). These dangerous falsehoods, such as the notion that the Rothschild family controls all of the world's banks, a secret, shadowy

CHAPTER 10

cabal rules the globe behind the scenes, and the existence of a blood libel all continue to thrive and gain further traction in U.S. society with support of mainstream politicians (Greenspan, 2020). As discussed in Chapter 3, "There are cultural arbiters ready to cancel anyone's careers over bigotry – except when, say, the rapper Ice Cube or the N.F.L. player DeSean Jackson, or the N.B.A. player Stephen Jackson posts anti-Semitic messages on social media" (Stephens, 2020, p. 1). In these situations, the outcry for justice is minimal, at best. Antisemitism certainly has not gone away; in many ways, anti-Semites have just found different dog whistles and modes of communication to get their hateful messages across. Stephens (2020) has posited that, "Anti-Semitism flourishes when adjacent hatreds – of 'globalists,' 'corporate media,' 'Hollywood' and so on – cease to be taboo. Anti-Semitism also flourishes when the purveyors of these adjacencies cease to be disreputable" (p. 1).

REFLECTION

I have gone to great lengths in this text to explain the need for a Jewish presence in the university diversity and multicultural classroom as well as the fields of multiculturalism and ethnic studies. By creating a branch of critical race theory called HebCrit, I have attempted to stick my foot in the front door to the multicultural club that has long been closed to the Jewish people. While I still feel that Jews are not really welcome in the field of multiculturalism, I have laid out, to the best of my ability, the arguments needed to persuade even the most oppositional of theoretical forces.

Over the past decade of academic research and writing, I have frequently been ignored, criticized, disregarded, and diminished in my attempt to place Jews in a position of acceptance and understanding. I was once even accused by an anonymous journal reviewer of attempting to appropriate Critical Race Theory to study "ethnically White Jews in the U.S." (I will admit that that one stung a little bit). That being said, I have long come into conflict with multiculturalists and critical race theorists about the place of Jews in racial/ethnic/multicultural studies, and I accept that with great pride.

I truly believe, as it has been mentioned in previous chapters, that my struggle with addressing the issues of Jewish positionality in multiculturalism is due to a general, persistent, fear of Jewish people speaking up. It is hard to put your neck on the line knowing that one's ancestors often had their throats slit for just that reason. It has been asserted that no group has been more victimized in history than the Jewish people (Black, 2004), yet when

Jews complain about antisemitism, they are often accused of playing the victim. It is essential that Jews' voices be heard. Antisemitic incidents must be identified in order to be overcome. Jews must continue to speak until people begin to listen and act.

WHERE DO WE GO FROM HERE?

The question now is, where do we go from here? My hope is that I have opened the door for future researchers to state, unequivocally and without hesitation, that Jews and the study of antisemitism belong in the study of multiculturalism. This sense of belonging does not mean, in any way, that other groups do not belong or should be focused on less; it just means that there is always room for one more seat at the table. Jews, just like Blacks, Latinxs, Asians, Indigenous Peoples, and members of the GLBTQ community, continue in their struggle against racism and injustice in U.S. society. Jews also need to continue to step up and stand alongside those fighting for equitable treatment and respect. If the Black Lives Matter protests have taught Americans anything, is that we all need to stand up for each other against racist forces of hatred that will continue to oppress without direct action. Just because the U.S. elected a new President in November 2020 does not mean that all the racial animus and discrimination against Blacks, Jews, refugees from Central America, and the GLBTQ community (just for starters) will magically disappear. We need to fight harder than ever to create a new status quo – one that does not change with every election.

For me, several threads were beginning to be pulled during my research for this book. For my next project, I would like to explore how internalized antisemitism affects U.S. Jews' embrasure of their own faith and how they see themselves. Data from my study on university professors and their experiences with antisemitism (see Chapter 8) has hinted at internalized antisemitism. Although some study participants mentioned how they were verbally and/or physically harassed and discriminated against in their youth just for being Jewish, they appear to minimize the acts as being of little importance. I firmly believe that U.S. Jews downplay (i.e., minimize) negative treatment such as this due to Jews having historically sought to assimilate and go unseen in U.S. society. I hope to work with academics experienced in psychology to facilitate this future research project. At this point, there is still a great amount of ground to cover in the study of the Jewish people. I look forward to seeing what comes next in my own personal journey as well as our collective journey as social justice advocates and multiculturalists.

REFERENCES

Abdul-Jabbar, K. (2020, July 14). Kareem Abdul-Jabbar: Where is the outrage over anti-Semitism in sports and Hollywood? *The Hollywood Reporter*. https://www.hollywoodreporter.com/news/kareem-abdul-jabbar-is-outrage-anti-semitism-sports-hollywood-1303210

Abramsky, S. (2018, October 27). The Pittsburgh synagogue shooting is the inevitable result of Trump's vile nationalism. *The Nation*. https://www.thenation.com/article/pittsburgh-shooting-result-trump-nationalism

Adams, M., Bell, A., Goodman, D. J., & Joshi, K. Y. (Eds.). (2016). *Teaching for diversity and social justice*. Routledge.

Adams, M., & Joshi, K. Y. (2016). Religious oppression. In M. Adams, L. A. Bell, D. J. Goodman, & K. Y. Joshi (Eds.), *Teaching for diversity and social justice* (3rd ed., pp. 255–297). Routledge.

Alarcón, W., Cruz, C., Jackson, L. G., Prieto, L., & Rodriguez-Arroyo, S. (2011). Compartiendo nuestras historias: Five testimonios of schooling and survival. *Journal of Latinos & Education, 10*(4), 369–381.

Alba, R. (2006). On the sociological significance on American Jewish experience: Boundary blurring, assimilation, and pluralism. *Sociology of Religion, 67*(4), 347–358.

Alexander, E. (1992). Multiculturalism's Jewish problem. *Academic Questions, 5*(4), 63–68.

Alexander, E. (1994). Multiculturalists and anti-Semitism. *Society, 31*(6), 58–64.

Alhadeff, C. J. (2014). *Viscous expectations: Justice, vulnerability, the ob-scene*. Penn State University Press.

Aliakbari1, M., & Faraji, E. (2011). Basic principles of critical pedagogy. *International Proceedings of Economics Development and Research, 17*, 77–85.

Altman, A. N., Inman, A. G., Fine, S. G., Ritter, H. A., & Howard, E. E. (2010). Exploration of Jewish ethnic identity. *Journal of Counseling & Development, 88*(2), 163–173.

AMCHA Initiative. (2015). *Antisemitic activity in 2015 at U.S. colleges and universities with the largest Jewish undergraduate populations*. http://www.amchainitiative.org/antisemitic-activity-schools-large-Jewish-report-2015

America's 25 Most Vibrant Congregations. (2009, April 3). *Newsweek*. http://www.newsweek.com/americas-25-most-vibrant-congregations-77069

Anderson, G. (2020, September 9). Responding to rise in campus anti-Semitism. *Inside Higher Ed*. https://www.insidehighered.com/news/2020/09/09/anti-semitism-rise-new-semester-starts?utm_source=Inside+Higher+Ed&utm_campaign=88ef879cf3-DNU_2020_COPY_02&utm_medium=email&utm_term=0_1fcbc04421-88ef879cf3-233914401&mc_cid=88ef879cf3&mc_eid=052e724749

Anti-Defamation League. (2017, April 24). U.S. anti-Semitic incidents spike 86 percent so far in 2017 after surging last year, ADL finds. https://www.adl.org/news/press-releases/us-anti-semitic-incidents-spike-86-percent-so-far-in-2017

Anti-Defamation League. (2019, April 30). Anti-Semitic incidents remained at near-historic levels in 2018; Assaults against Jews more than doubled. https://www.adl.org/news/press-releases/anti-semitic-incidents-remained-at-near-historic-levels-in-2018-assaults

Anti-Defamation League. (2020, July 16). Black-Jewish alliance of ADL issues statement on recent spate of antisemitic social media posts by celebrities. https://philadelphia.adl.org/black-jewish-alliance-of-adl-issues-statement-on-recent-spate-of-antisemitic-social-media-posts-by-celebrities/

REFERENCES

Arendt, F., & Northup, T. (2015). Effects of long-term exposure to news stereotypes on implicit and explicit attitudes. *International Journal of Communication, 9*, 2370–2390.

Armus, T. (2020, November 3). 'Trump' and 'MAGA' spray-painted on gravestones in Michigan Jewish cemetery. *The Washington Post*. https://www.washingtonpost.com/nation/2020/11/03/michigan-jewish-cemetery-trump-maga/

Askar, A. (2015). On the relationship between Zionism and Judaism. *Palestine-Israel Journal of Politics, Economics & Culture, 20/21*(4/1), 67–74.

Astor, M. (2018, February 27). Anti-Semitic incidents surged 57 percent in 2017, report finds. *The New York Times*. https://www.nytimes.com/2018/02/27/us/anti-semitism-adl-report.html

Au, W. (Ed.). (2014). *Rethinking multicultural education: Teaching for racial and cultural justice*. Rethinking Schools, Ltd.

Ayers, W., Hunt, J. A., & Quinn, T. (1998). *Teaching for social justice: A democracy and education reader*. The New Press.

Baker, L. M., Lyons, H. Z., Schlosser, L. Z., & Talleyrand, R. M. (2007). Racism, antisemitism, and the schism between Blacks and Jews in the United States: A pilot intergroup encounter program. *Journal of Multicultural Counseling and Development, 35*(2), 116–128.

Banks, J. A. (1992). Multicultural education: For freedom's sake. *Educational Leadership, 49*(4), 32–36.

Banks, J. A. (2005). The social construction of difference and the quest for educational equity. In Z. Leonardo (Ed.), *Critical pedagogy and race* (pp. 93–110). Blackwell Publishing Ltd.

Banks, J. A. (2016). Multicultural education: Characteristics and goals. In J. A. Banks & C. A. Banks (Eds.), *Multicultural education: Issues and perspectives* (9th ed., pp. 2–23). Wiley.

Banks, J. A., & Banks, C. A. (2016). *Multicultural education: Issues and perspectives* (9th ed.). Wiley.

Barall, K. P., & Paolozzi, A. (2020, March 11). Shocking ignorance about the Holocaust illustrates the need to pass the Never Again Education Act. *The Hill*. https://thehill.com/blogs/congress-blog/education/487058-shocking-ignorance-about-the-holocaust-illustrates-the-need-to

Barton, E. (2002). Resources for discourse analysis in composition studies. *Style, 36*(4), 575–595.

Baskind, S. (2007). The Fockerized Jew? Questioning Jewishness as cool in American popular entertainment. *Shofar: An Interdisciplinary Journal of Jewish Studies, 25*(4), 3–17.

Beam, C. B. (2007). A conversation on the semantic pedagogy of "Whiteness." *ETC: A Review of General Semantics, 64*(3), 209–217.

Beaumont, P. (2016, March 31). Israel-Palestine: Outlook bleak as wave of violence passes six-month mark. *The Guardian*. https://www.theguardian.com/world/2016/mar/31/israel-palestine-violence-knife-attacks-west-bank-gaza

Beaumont-Thomas, B. (2020, July 24). Wiley posts antisemitic tweets, likening Jews to Ku Klux Klan. *The Guardian*. https://www.theguardian.com/music/2020/jul/24/wiley-accused-of-antisemitism-after-likening-jews-to-ku-klux-klan

Beckwith, L. (2011). Antisemitism at the University of California. *Journal for the Study of Antisemitism, 3*(2), 443–462.

Belding-Zidon, M. (2020, June 10). Stop using Israel as an excuse not to support Black lives matter. *Jewish Telegraphic Agency*. https://www.jta.org/2020/06/10/opinion/stop-using-israel-as-an-excuse-not-to-support-black-lives-matter

Bell, D., & Edmonds, E. (1993). Students as teachers, teachers as learners. *Michigan Law Review, 91*(8), 2025–2052.

Benton, B. (2015). Lamination as slamination: Irwin R. Schyster and the construction of antisemitism in professional wrestling. *The Journal of Popular Culture, 48*(2), 399–412.

REFERENCES

Berinsky, A. J., & Mendelberg, T. (2005). The indirect effects of discredited stereotypes in judgments of Jewish leaders. *American Journal of Political Science, 49*(4), 845–864.

Bernstein, D. (2012, July 30). Academic tradition demands more evenhanded treatment of Israel. *The Chronicle of Higher Education, 58*(42). http://chronicle.com/article/Academic-Tradition-Demands/133183/

Bertman, S. (2009). The antisemitic origin of Michelangelo's Horned Moses. *Shofar: An Interdisciplinary Journal of Jewish Studies, 27*(4), 95–107.

Bever, L. (2015, March 6). Just before suicide, Missouri politician fretted about rumors he was Jewish. *The Washington Post*. http://www.washingtonpost.com/news/morning-mix/wp/2015/03/06/the-tragic-last-moments-before-a-missouri-politician-took-his-life-upset-about-rumors-that-he-was-jewish/

Biale, D. (1998). The melting pot and beyond: Jews and the politics of American identity. In D. Biale, M. Galchinsky, & S. Heschel (Eds.), *Insider/outsider: American Jews and multiculturalism* (pp. 17–33). University of California Press.

Biale, D., Galchinsky, M., & Heschel, S. (1998). Introduction: The dialectic of Jewish enlightenment. In D. Biale, M. Galchinsky, & S. Heschel (Eds.), *Insider/outsider: American Jews and multiculturalism* (pp. 1–13). University of California Press.

Black, T. (2004, March). Why are the Jews the 'chosen' victims? *History Today*. https://www.historytoday.com/archive/why-are-jews-%E2%80%98chosen%E2%80%99-victims

Blake, J. (2020, July 18). Despite recent anti-Semitic comments, Jews and Black people have long been allies. *CNN*. https://www.cnn.com/2020/07/18/us/anti-semitic-comments-blacks-jews-blake/index.html

Blumenfeld, W. J. (2006a). Christian privilege and the promotion of "secular" and not-so "secular" mainline Christianity in public schooling and in the larger society. *Equity & Excellence in Education, 39*(3), 195–210.

Blumenfeld, W. J. (2006b). Outside/inside/between sides: An investigation of Ashkenazi Jewish perceptions on their "race." *Multicultural Perspectives, 8*(3), 11–18.

Blumenfeld, W. J., & Jaekel, K. (2012). Exploring levels of Christian privilege awareness among preservice teachers. *Journal of Social Issues, 68*(1), 128–144.

Botelho, M. J., & Rudman, M. K. (2009). *Critical multicultural analysis of children's literature: Mirrors, windows, and doors*. Routledge.

Bowden, C., & Galindo-Gonzalez, S. (2015). Interviewing when you're not face-to-face: The use of email interviews in a phenomenological study. *International Journal of Doctoral Studies, 10*, 79–93.

Bowden, J. (2020, February 12). Study: White nationalist propaganda distribution on college campuses nearly doubled in 2019. *The Hill*. https://thehill.com/blogs/blog-briefing-room/news/482702-study-white-nationalist-propaganda-distribution-on-college

Brand, J., & Falsey, J. (Executive Producers). (1990–1995). *Northern exposure* [TV series]. CBS.

Brayboy, B. M. J. (2005). Toward a Tribal critical race theory in education. *The Urban Review, 37*(5), 425–446.

Bright, K. S., Kauffman, M., & Crane, D. (Executive Producers). (1994–2004). *Friends* [TV series]. NBC.

Brodkin, K. (2000). *How Jews became White folks and what that says about race in America*. Rutgers University Press.

Brook, V. (1999a). The Americanization of Molly: How mid-fifties TV homogenized The Goldbergs (and got "Berg-larized" in the process). *Cinema Journal, 38*(4), 45–67.

REFERENCES

Brook, V. (1999b). From the cozy to the carceral: Trans-formations of ethnic space in The Goldbergs and Seinfeld. *Velvet Light Trap, 44*, 54–67.

Buchbinder, D. (2008). Enter the schlemiel: The emergence of inadequate or incompetent masculinities in recent film and television. *Canadian Review of American Studies, 38*(2), 227–245.

Byers, M., & Krieger, R. (2005). Beyond binaries and condemnation: Opening new theoretical spaces in Jewish television studies. *Culture, Theory and Critique, 46*(2), 131–145.

Cabrera, N. L. (2018). Where is the racial theory in critical race theory? A constructive criticism of the crits. *The Review of Higher Education, 42*(1), 209–233.

Campus Safety. (2020, May 12). Antisemitic incidents hit all-time high in 2019. *Campus Safety Magazine*. https://www.campussafetymagazine.com/news/antisemitic-incidents-hit-all-time-high-in-2019/

Cannon, B. (2014, December 4). *Jews, white privilege and the fight against racism in America.* http://www.haaretz.com/jewish-world/the-jewish-thinker/1.629888

Cantone, J. A., & Weiner, R. L. (2017). Religion at work: Evaluating hostile work environment religious discrimination claims. *Psychology, Public Policy, and Law, 23*(3), 351–366.

Cantor, M. G. (1991). The American family on television: From Molly Goldberg to Bill Cosby. *Journal of Comparative Family Studies, 22*(2), 205–216.

Caro, I. (2015). Anti-Semitism, anti-Zionism, and Israeli-Palestinian conflict from 2000 to 2014: Some visions from Latin American southern cone. *TRAMES: A Journal of the Humanities & Social Sciences, 19*(3), 289–307.

Castagno, A. (2005). Extending the bounds of race and racism: Indigenous women and the persistence of the Black–White paradigm of race. *Urban Review, 37*(5), 447–468.

Chait, J. (2020, September 23). Report: Trump said Jews are 'Only in it for themselves.' *Intelligencer*. https://nymag.com/intelligencer/2020/09/trump-anti-semite-said-jews-are-only-in-it-for-themselves-racism.html

Chanbonpin, K. D. (2015). Between black and White: The coloring of Asian Americans. *Washington University Global Studies Law Review, 14*(4), 637–663.

Chanes, J. A. (1999). Antisemitism and Jewish security in contemporary America: Why can't Jews take yes for an answer? In R. Rosenberg Farber & C. I. Waxman (Eds.), *Jews in America: A contemporary reader* (pp. 124–150). Brandeis University Press.

Chang, R. S. (1993). Toward an Asian American legal scholarship: Critical race theory, post-structuralism, and narrative space. *California Law Review, 81*(5), 1243–1993.

Chou, H. (2007). Multicultural teacher education: Toward a culturally responsible pedagogy. *Essays in Education, 21*, 139–162.

Clanton, D. (2013, May 1). The (not-so) Jewish tao of Howard Wolowitz. *Moment Magazine*. www.momentmag.com/the-not-so-jewish-tao-of-howard-wolowitz/

Cochran-Smith, M., Gleeson, A. M., & Mitchell, K. (2010). Teacher education for social justice: What's pupil learning got to do with it? *Berkeley Review of Education, 1*(1), 35–61.

Cohen, F. (2010). Educating about antisemitism through personal stories. *Journal for the Study of Antisemitism, 2*(2), 471–475.

Cohen, F., Harber, K. D., Jussim, L., & Bhasin, G. (2009). Modern anti-Semitism and anti-Israeli attitudes. *Journal of Personality and Social Psychology, 97*(2), 290–306.

Cohen, J. E. (2010). Perceptions of anti-Semitism among American Jews, 2000–05: A survey analysis. *Political Psychology, 31*(1), 85–107.

Cohen, M. A. (2018, April 9). The unmentioned motive in Parkland: Anti-Semitism. *The Boston Globe*. https://www.bostonglobe.com/opinion/2018/04/09/the-unmentioned-motive-parkland-anti-semitism/2oXfMvNBEFP0zyIG93tTpL/story.html

REFERENCES

Cohen, S. (2020, July 11). Falling for Farrakhan? How Black-Jewish relations keep stumbling over one man. *Forbes.* https://www.forbes.com/sites/sethcohen/2020/07/11/falling-for-farrakhan/#71f5ff195a2f

Cohen Ferris, M. (2004). Feeding the Jewish soul in the Delta diaspora. *Southern Cultures, 10*(3), 52–85.

Crandall, C. S., Miller, J. M., & White II, M. H. (2018). Changing norms following the 2016 U.S. Presidential election: The Trump effect on prejudice. *Social Psychological and Personality Science, 9*(2), 186–192.

Cravatts, R. (2011). Antisemitism and the campus left. *Journal for the Study of Antisemitism, 3*(2), 407–442.

Crenson, M. (2006). Choosing to be chosen: Hispanic New Mexicans intrigued by hints of a hidden Jewish past. *Albuquerque Journal.* http://www.abqjournal.com/news/state/appast12-09-06.htm

Cresswell, J. W. (2007). *Qualitative inquiry and research design* (2nd ed.). Sage.

Cresswell, J. W., & Miller, D. L. (2000). Determining validity in qualitative inquiry. *Theory into Practice, 39*(3), 124–130.

Cummins, J. (2001, June). *The Jewish child in picture books?* Paper presented at the 36th Annual Convention of the Association of Jewish Libraries, La Jolla, CA.

Darder, A. (2015). Foreword. In P. W. Orelus & R. Brock (Eds.), *Interrogating critical pedagogy: The voices of educators of color in the movement* (pp. xi–xiv). Routledge.

Darder, A., Mayo, P., & Paraskeva, J. (2016). The internationalization of critical pedagogy: An introduction. In A. Darder, P. Mayo, & J. Paraskeva (Eds.), *International critical pedagogy reader* (pp. 1–14). Routledge.

David, L., & Seinfeld, J. (Executive Producers). (1989–1998). *Seinfeld* [TV series]. NBC.

Davis-Delano, L. R., Gone, J. P., & Fryberg, S. A. (2020). The psychosocial effects of Native American mascots: A comprehensive review of empirical research findings. *Race Ethnicity and Education, 23*(5), 613–633.

Delgado, R., & Stefancic, J. (2017). *Critical race theory: An introduction* (3rd ed.). NYU Press.

DiAngelo, R. (2016). *What does it mean to be white? Developing white racial literacy* (rev. ed.). Peter Lang Publishing, Inc.

Dinnerstein, L. (1994). *Antisemitism in America.* Oxford University Press.

Dixson, A. D., & Anderson, C. R. (2018). Where are we? Critical race theory in education 20 years later. *Peabody Journal of Education, 93*(1), 121–131.

Dollinger, M. (2018). *Black power, Jewish politics: Reinventing the alliance in the 1960s.* Brandeis University Press.

Donaghue, E. (2020, November, 16). Hate crime murders surged to record high in 2019, FBI data show. *CBS News.* https://www.cbsnews.com/news/hate-crime-fbi-statistics-show-murders-rose-2019/

Drescher, S. (1993). The role of Jews in the transatlantic slave trade. *Immigrants & Minorities: Historical Studies in Ethnicity, Migration and Diaspora, 12*(2), 113–125.

Earls, A. (2019). African Americans have mixed opinions and often no opinions on Israel. *Lifeway.* https://factsandtrends.net/tag/jews/

Efron, J. M. (2013). Jewish genetic origins in the context of past historical and anthropological inquiries. *Human Biology, 85*(6), 901–918.

Eisner, J. (2019, March 19). Why we don't talk about Jewish poverty – and why we should. *Forward.* https://forward.com/culture/421071/why-we-dont-talk-about-jewish-poverty-and-why-we-should/

English, D. (Executive Producer). (1988–1998). *Murphy Brown* [TV series]. CBS.

REFERENCES

Estrin, D. (2020, April 21). New report notes rise in coronavirus-linked anti-Semitic hate speech. *NPR*. https://www.npr.org/sections/coronavirus-live-updates/2020/04/21/839748857/new-report-notes-rise-in-coronavirus-linked-anti-semitic-hate-speech

Faber, E. (1998). *Jews, slaves, and the slave trade: Setting the record straight*. New York University Press.

Fairchild, E. E. (2009). Christian privilege, history, and trends in U.S. religion. *New Directions for Student Services, 125*, 5–11.

Fairclough, N. (2001). The dialectics of discourse. *TEXTUS, 14*(2), 231–242.

Fairclough, N. (2005). Critical discourse analysis. *Marges Linguistiques, 9*, 76–94.

Farber, B. A., & Poleg, A. (2019). Campus diversity, Jewishness, and antisemitism. *Journal of Clinical Psychology, 75*, 2034–2048.

Federal Bureau of Investigation. (2020, November 16). *2019 Hate crime statistics*. https://ucr.fbi.gov/hate-crime/2019/topic-pages/victims

Feingold, H. (2017). *Jewish power in America: Myth and reality*. Routledge.

Fitzgerald, T. (2019, May 17). How do 'The Big Bang Theory' series finale ratings rank all time? *Forbes.com*. https://www.forbes.com/sites/tonifitzgerald/2019/05/17/how-does-the-big-bang-theory-series-finale-ratings-rank-all-time/#6d17abdf386d

Floyd, M. H. (2006). The production of prophetic books in the early Second Temple period. In M. Floyd & R. D. Haak (Eds.), *Prophets, prophecy, and prophetic texts in Second Temple Judaism* (pp. 276–297). T & T Clark International.

Foner, P. S. (1975). Black-Jewish relations in the opening years of the twentieth century. *Phylon, 36*(4), 359–367.

Fox, D. (2018). "We are the first temple": Fact and affect in American Jews' emergent genetic narrative. *Shofar: An Interdisciplinary Journal of Jewish Studies, 36*(1), 74–107.

Freedman, J. (2005). Transgressions of a model minority. *Shofar: An Interdisciplinary Journal of Jewish Studies, 23*(4), 69–97.

Freidenreich, H. P. (2007). Joining the faculty club: Jewish women academics in the United States. *Nashim: A Journal of Jewish Women's Studies & Gender Issues, 13*, 68–101.

Freire, P., & Macedo, D. (1998). Literacy: Reading the word and the world. *Thinking, 14*(1), 8–10.

Friedman, E. (2016). Recognition gaps in the Israeli-Palestinian conflict: The people-state and self-other axes. *Journal of Language & Politics, 15*(2), 193–214.

Fryberg, S. A., Markus, H. R., Oyserman, D., & Stone. J. M. (2008). Of warrior chiefs and Indian princesses: The psychological consequences of American Indian mascots. *Basic and Applied Social Psychology, 39*(3), 208–218.

Furman, A. (2000). *Contemporary Jewish American writers and the multicultural dilemma: Return of the exiled*. Syracuse University Press.

Gabriel, M., & Goldberg, E. (Directors). (1995). *Pocahontas* [Film]. Disney.

Galchinsky, M. (1994). Glimpsing golus in the golden land: Jews and multiculturalism in America. *Judaism: A Quarterly Journal of Jewish Life, 43*(4), 360–368.

Gerson, J. M. (2018). Gender theory, Intersectionality and new understandings of Jewishness. *Journal of Jewish Identities, 11*(1), 5–16.

Gerstmann, E. (2020, September 9). Hate crimes against Jewish students are at an all-time high. *Forbes*. https://www.forbes.com/sites/evangerstmann/2020/09/09/hate-crimes-against-jewish-students-are-at-an-all-time-high/?fbclid=IwAR3aw0QsFpBi8ugl2kbp2XzLWnZ50kG0kR5ShBdjqWGMWHqB2q_-q3h42j0&sh=7eb0a2e9632f

Ghanem, A. (2016). Israel's second-class citizens: Arabs in Israel and the struggle for equal rights. *Foreign Affairs, 95*(4), 37–42.

REFERENCES

Ghumman, S., & Jackson, L. (2008). Between a cross and a hard place: Religious identifiers and employability. *Journal of Workplace Rights, 13*(3), 259–279.

Ghumman, S., Ryan, A. M., Barclay, L. A., & Markel, K. S. (2013). Religious discrimination in the workplace: A review. *Journal of Business and Psychology, 28*, 439–454.

Gilman, S. L. (1994). The Jewish nose: Are Jews White? Or, the history of the nose job. In L. J. Silberstein & R. L. Cohn (Eds.), *The other in Jewish thought and history: Constructions of Jewish culture and identity* (pp. 364–401). New York University Press.

Gilman, S. L. (2003). "We're not Jews": Imagining Jewish history and Jewish bodies in contemporary multicultural literature. *Modern Judaism, 23*(2), 126–155.

Giroux, H. A. (1997). White squall: Resistance and the pedagogy of whiteness. *Cultural Studies, 11*(3), 376–389.

Giroux, H. A. (2006). Reading hurricane Katrina: Race, class, and the biopolitics of disposability. *College Literature, 33*(3), 171–196.

Glauz-Todrank, A. E. (2014). Race, religion, or ethnicity? Situating Jews in the American scene. *Religion Compass, 8*(10), 303–316.

Glenn, S. A. (2010). "Funny, you don't look Jewish": Visual stereotypes and the making of modern Jewish identity. In S. A. Glenn & N. B. Sokoloff (Eds.), *Boundaries of Jewish identity* (pp. 64–90). University of Washington Press.

Goldberg, B., & Goldberg, S. (2000). *I'm next: The strange journey of America's most unlikely superhero.* Crown Publishing.

Goldstein, D. M., & Hall, K. (2017). Postelection surrealism and nostalgic racism in the hands of Donald Trump. *Hau: Journal of Ethnographic Theory, 7*(1), 397–406.

Goldstein, E. L. (2006). *The price of whiteness: Jews, race, and American identity.* Princeton University Press.

Gonzalez-Sobrino, B., & Goss, D. R. (2019). Exploring the mechanisms of racialization beyond the Black–White binary. *Ethnic and Racial Studies, 42*(4), 505–510.

Grant, C. A., & Zwier, E. (2011). Intersectionality and student outcomes: Sharpening the struggle against racism, sexism, classism, ableism, heterosexism, nationalism, and linguistic, religious, and geographical discrimination in teaching and learning. *Multicultural Perspectives, 13*(4), 181–188.

Green, E. (2016, December 5). Are Jews White? *The Atlantic.* https://www.theatlantic.com/politics/archive/2016/12/are-jews-white/509453/

Greene, R. A. (2018). CNN poll reveals depth of anti-Semitism in Europe. *CNN.* https://edition.cnn.com/interactive/2018/11/europe/antisemitism-poll-2018-intl/

Greenberg, C. (1998). Pluralism and its discontents: The case of Blacks and Jews. In D. Biale, M. Galchinsky, & S. Heschel (Eds.), *Insider/outsider: American Jews and multiculturalism* (pp. 55–87). University of California Press.

Greenberg, C. (2013). "I'm not White – I'm Jewish": The racial politics of American Jews. In E. Sicher (Ed.), *Race, color, identity: Rethinking discourses about "Jews" in the twenty-first century* (pp. 35–55). Berghahn Books.

Greenberg, C. L. (2010). *Troubling the waters: Black-Jewish relations in the American century.* Princeton University Press.

Greenspan, R. E. (2020, October 24). QAnon builds on centuries of anti-Semitic conspiracy theories that put Jewish people at risk. *Insider.* https://www.insider.com/qanon-conspiracy-theory-anti-semitism-jewish-racist-believe-save-children-2020-10

Grigsby Bates, K. (2020, October 21). Is Trump really that racist? *NPR.* https://www.npr.org/2020/10/19/925385389/is-trump-really-that-racist

REFERENCES

Grinberg, R. A. (2014). Neither 'sissy' boy nor patrician man: New York intellectuals and the construction of American Jewish masculinity. *American Jewish History, 98*(3), 127–151.

Gross, N., & Simmons, S. (2009). The religiosity of American college and university professors. *Sociology of Religion, 70*(2), 101–129.

Gross, Z., & Rutland, S. D. (2014). Combatting antisemitism in the school playground: An Australian case study. *Patterns of Prejudice, 48*(3), 309–330.

Hackman, H. W. (2005). Five essential components for social justice education. *Equity & Excellence in Education, 38*(2), 103–109.

Haltiwanger, J. (2020, September 30). Trump has repeatedly been endorsed by white supremacist groups and other far-right extremists, and they've looked to him as a source of encouragement. *Business Insider*. https://www.businessinsider.com/trumps-history-of-support-from-white-supremacist-far-right-groups-2020-9

Harris, R. S., & Shichtman, M. B. (2018). BDS, credibility, and the challenge to the academy. *Shofar, 36*(1), 161–182.

Harro, B. (2000). The cycle of socialization. In M. Adams (Ed.), *Readings for diversity and social justice: An anthology on racism, antisemitism, sexism, heterosexism, ableism, and classism* (pp. 15–21). Routledge.

Hauslohner, A. (2018, May 11). Hate crimes jump for fourth straight year in largest U.S. cities, study shows. *The Washington Post*. https://www.washingtonpost.com/news/post-nation/wp/2018/05/11/hate-crime-rates-are-still-on-the-rise/?utm_term=.c6c29e75a735

Hayden, M. E. (2017, November 2). Anti-Semitism rising in 'alt-right' era, new study shows. *Newsweek*. http://www.newsweek.com/anti-semitism-rising-alt-right-era-study-699218

Haynes, M. (2003). Vive la Différance: Jewish women teachers' constructions of ethnicity and identity and their experiences of anti-Semitism in secondary schools. *Race, Ethnicity and Education, 6*(1), 51–70.

Haynes Writer, J., & Baptiste, H. P. (2009). Realizing students' everyday realities: Community analysis as a model for social justice. *Journal of Praxis in Multicultural Education, 4*(1), 65–82.

Haynes Writer, J., & Chavez Chavez, R. (2001). Storied lives, dialog –> Retro-reflections: Melding critical multicultural education and critical race theory for pedagogical transformation. *Studies in Media & Information Literacy Education, 1*(4), 1–16.

Heath, S. B., & Street, B. V. (2008). *On ethnography: Approaches to language and literacy research*. Teachers College Press.

Henley, J. (2019, February 15). Antisemitism rising sharply across Europe, latest figures show. *The Guardian*. https://www.theguardian.com/news/2019/feb/15/antisemitism-rising-sharply-across-europe-latest-figures-show

Hershberger, P., & Kavanaugh, K. (2017). Comparing appropriateness and equivalence of email interviews to phone interviews in qualitative research on reproductive decisions. *Applied Nursing Research, 37*, 50–54.

Hill, J. (2020, July 13). The anti-Semitism we didn't see. *The Atlantic*. https://www.theatlantic.com/ideas/archive/2020/07/desean-jacksons-blind-spot-and-mine/614095/?fbclid=IwAR2jICBbPdkfLeRIFtQGh69xugaqG6FGvmjx79Hg-ui2Y9eP-s5kt5Br8lFE

Hirsh, D. (2018). *Contemporary left antisemitism*. Routledge.

Hochman, A. (2018). Racialization: A defense of the concept. *Ethnic and Racial Studies, 42*(8), 1245–1262.

REFERENCES

Hollinger, D. A. (2004). Rich, powerful, and smart: Jewish overrepresentation should be explained instead of avoided or mystified. *The Jewish Quarterly Review, 94*(4), 595–602.

Hodges, B. D., Kuper, A., & Reeves, S. (2008). Qualitative research: Discourse analysis. *British Medical Journal, 337*, 570–572.

Huckin, T., Andrus, J., & Clary-Lemon, J. (2012). Critical discourse analysis and rhetoric and composition. *College Composition and Communication, 64*(1), 107–129.

Hurley, R. J., Jensen, J., Weaver, A., & Dixon, T. (2015). Viewer ethnicity matters: Black crime in TV news and its impact on decisions regarding public policy. *Journal of Social Issues, 71*(1), 155–170.

Hyman, P. (2002). Gender and the shaping of modern Jewish identities. *Jewish Social Studies, 8*(2/3), 153–161.

Ibrahim, D., & Wolf, M. A. (2011). Television news, Jewish youth, and self-image. In P. M. Lester (Ed.), *Images that injure: Pictorial stereotypes in the media* (3rd ed., pp. 297–310). Praeger.

Ioffe, J. (2018, October 27). How much responsibility does Trump bear for the synagogue shooting in Pittsburgh? *The Washington Post.* https://www.washingtonpost.com/outlook/2018/10/28/how-much-responsibility-does-trump-bear-synagogue-shooting-pittsburgh/?utm_term=.2e4454c00f59

James, N. (2007). The use of email interviewing as a qualitative method of inquiry in educational research. *British Educational Research Journal, 33*(6), 963–976.

Jarus, O. (2016, August 16). Ancient Israel: A brief history. *LiveScience.* https://www.livescience.com/55774-ancient-israel.html

Jaschik, S. (2009, December 28). The lost tribe. *Inside Higher Ed.* https://www.insidehighered.com/news/2009/12/28/jews

Jewish Population. (2020). Jewish population in the United States by state. *Jewish Virtual Library.* https://www.jewishvirtuallibrary.org/jewish-population-in-the-united-states-by-state

Jewish Virtual Library. (2019). Ancient Jewish history: Jews of the Middle East. https://www.jewishvirtuallibrary.org/jews-of-the-middle-east

Johnson, G. (1996, October 29). Scholars debate roots of Yiddish, migration of Jews. *The New York Times.* https://www.nytimes.com/1996/10/29/science/scholars-debate-roots-of-yiddish-migration-of-jews.html

Johnson, R. B., & Christensen, L. B. (2012). *Educational research: Quantitative, qualitative, and mixed approaches* (4th ed.). Sage Publications.

Jones-Correa, M. (Winter, 2000–2001). The origins and diffusion of racial restrictive covenants. *Political Science Quarterly, 115*(4), 541–568.

Jupp, J. C., Berry, T. R., & Lensmire, T. J. (2016). Second-wave White teacher identity studies. *Review of Educational Research, 86*(4), 1151–1191.

Jupp, J. C., & Slattery, G. P., Jr. (2010). Committed White male teachers and identifications: Toward creative identifications and a "second wave" of White identity studies. *Curriculum Inquiry, 40*(3), 454–474.

Jupp, J. C., Slattery, G. P., Jr. (2012). "Becoming" teachers of inner-city students: Identification creativity and curriculum wisdom of committed White male teachers. *Urban Education, 47*(1), 280–311.

Jupp, J. C., & Sleeter, C. E. (2016). Interview of Christine Sleeter on multicultural education: Past, present, and key future directions. *National Youth-At-Risk Journal, 1*(2), 8–26.

Kahn, S. M. (2013). Who are the Jews? New formulations of an age-old question. *Human Biology, 85*(6), 919–924.

REFERENCES

Kaplan, S. (2003). If there are no races, how can Jews be a "race"? *Journal of Modern Jewish Studies, 2*(1), 79–96.

Karatas, K., & Oral, B. (2015). Teachers' perceptions on culturally responsiveness in education. *Journal of Ethnic and Cultural Studies, 2*(2), 47–57.

Katz, E. B., & Lipstadt, D. (2020, July 18). Far more unites Black and Jewish Americans than divides them. *CNN.* https://www.cnn.com/2020/07/18/opinions/black-celebrities-anti-semitism-anti-racism-katz-lipstadt/index.html

Keesing-Styles, L. (2003). The relationship between critical pedagogy and assessment in teacher education. *Radical Pedagogy, 5*(1). http://www.radicalpedagogy.org/radicalpedagogy/The_Relationship_between_Critical_Pedagogy_and_Assessment_in_Teacher_Education.html

Kelkar, K. (2017, September 16). *PBS NewsHour. How a shifting definition of "White" helped shape U.S. immigration policy.* https://www.pbs.org/newshour/nation/white-u-s-immigration-policy

Kelman, A. Y., Tapper, A. H., Fonseca, I., & Saperstein, A. (2019). Counting inconsistencies: An analysis of American Jewish population studies, with a focus on Jews of color. *The Jews of Color Field Building Initiative.* https://jewsofcolorfieldbuilding.org/wp-content/uploads/2019/05/Counting-Inconsistencies-052119.pdf

King, J. E. (1991). Dysconscious racism: Ideology, identity, and the miseducation of teachers. *Journal of Negro Education, 60*(2), 133–145.

King, R. D., & Weiner, M. F. (2007). Group position, collective threat, and American anti-Semitism. *Social Problems, 54*(1), 47–77.

Kirchick, J. (2018, June). The rise of Black anti-Semitism. *Commentary Magazine.* https://www.commentarymagazine.com/articles/james-kirchick/rise-black-anti-semitism/

Kirka, D. (2020, July 27). Twitter faces 48-hour boycott over anti-Semitic posts by rapper Wiley. *Fortune.* https://fortune.com/2020/07/27/twitter-boycott-wiley-anti-semitic-posts-instagram/

Korn, B. W. (1961). Jews and Negro slavery in the old south, 1789–1865. *Publications of the American Jewish Historical Society, 50*(3), 151–201.

Kramer, M. (1985, February 4). Blacks and Jews. *New York Magazine.* https://nymag.com/news/features/49091/

Kremer, S. L. (2001). Contemporary Jewish American writers and the multicultural dilemma: Return of the exiled (review). *American Jewish History, 89*(3), 318–320.

Kulwin, C. M. (2020, January 19). What Jewish and black people owe each other. *Los Angeles Times.* https://www.latimes.com/opinion/story/2020-01-19/jews-african-americans-civil-rights-movement

Kunzelman, M. (2018, May 7). *Report: Millions of tweets spread anti-Semitic messages.* The Associated Press. https://apnews.com/9bc19992b5294dc887a37e00a3e652cd

Ladson-Billings, G. J. (1996). "Your blues ain't like mine": Keeping issues of race and racism on the multicultural agenda. *Theory into Practice, 35*(4), 248–255.

Ladson-Billings, G. J. (1998). Just what is critical race theory and what's it doing in a nice field like education? *Qualitative Studies in Education, 11*(1), 7–24.

Ladson-Billings, G. J. (1999). Preparing teachers for diverse student populations: A critical race theory perspective. *Review of Research in Education, 24,* 211–247.

Ladson-Billings, G. J. (2018). The social funding of race: The role of schooling. *Peabody Journal of Education, 93*(1), 90–105.

Ladson-Billings, G., & Tate, W. F. (1995). Toward a critical race theory of education. *Teachers College Record, 97*(1), 47–68.

REFERENCES

Langman, P. F. (1995). Including Jews in multiculturalism. *Journal of Multicultural Counseling & Development, 23*(4), 222–236.

Langman, P. F. (1999). *Jewish issues in multiculturalism: A handbook for educators and clinicians.* Jason Aronson, Inc.

Langman, P. F. (2000). Assessment issues with Jewish clients. In R. H. Dana (Ed.), *Handbook of cross-cultural and multicultural personality assessment* (pp. 647–688). Laurence Erlbaum Associates, Inc.

Lasson, K. (2010). Campus antisemitism. *Journal for the Study of Antisemitism, 2*(2), 451–458.

Lawrence, B. (Executive Producer). (2001–2010). *Scrubs* [TV series]. NBC.

Lea, V., & Sims, E. J. (2008). Undoing Whiteness in the classroom: Different origins, shared commitment. In J. K. Kincheloe & S. R. Steinberg (Eds.), *Undoing Whiteness in the classroom: Critical educultural teaching approaches for social justice activism* (pp. 1–28). Peter Lang.

Leff, L. (2019). *Well worth saving: American universities' life-and-death decisions on refugees from Nazi Europe.* Yale University Press.

Lensmire, T. J., McManimon, S. K., Tierney, J. D., Lee-Nichols, M. E., Casey, Z. A., Lensmire, A, & Davis, B. M. (2013). McIntosh as synecdoche: How teacher education's focus on White privilege undermines antiracism. *Harvard Educational Review, 83*(3), 410–431.

Leonardo, Z. (2005). *Critical pedagogy and race.* Blackwell Publishing.

Levine-Rasky, C. (2008). White privilege: Jewish women's writing and the instability of categories. *Journal of Modern Jewish Studies, 7*(1), 51–66.

Lew, J. (2006). Burden of acting neither White nor Black: Asian American identities and achievement in urban schools. *Urban Review: Issues and Ideas in Public Education, 38*(5), 335–352.

Lightman, E. (2010). Antisemitism at the University of Toronto. *Journal for the Study of Antisemitism, 2*(2), 363–376.

Liu, A. (2009). Critical race theory, Asian Americans, and higher education: A review of research. *InterActions: UCLA Journal of Education and Information Studies, 5*(2). https://escholarship.org/uc/item/98h4n45j

Lorre, C., & Prady, B. (Creators). (2007–2019). *The Big Bang Theory* [TV series]. Chuck Lorre Productions; Warner Bros. Television; CBS Television.

Love, D. (2020, July 19). Calling out racism and anti-Semitism is a responsibility. *CNN.* https://www.cnn.com/2020/07/19/opinions/racism-anti-semitism-blm-nick-cannon-love/index.html

Lozano, A. (2017, January/February). Breaking the Black/White binary in higher education leadership. *About Campus, 21*(6), 27–21.

MacDonald-Dennis, C. (2006). Understanding anti-Semitism and its impact: A new framework for conceptualizing Jewish identity. *Equity & Excellence in Education, 39*(3), 267–278.

Maddux, W. M., Galinsky, A. D., Cuddy, A. J. C., & Polifroni, M. (2008). When being a model minority is good…and bad: Realistic threat explains negativity toward Asian Americans. *Personality and Social Psychology Bulletin, 34*, 74–89. doi:10.1177/0146167207309195

Maizels, L. (2011). On whiteness and the Jews. *Journal for the Study of Antisemitism, 3*(2), 463–488.

Marable, M. (1992). US commentary: At the end of the rainbow. *Race & Class, 34*(2), 75–81.

Marshall, C., & Rossman, G. B. (2006). *Designing qualitative research.* Sage Publications, Inc.

125

REFERENCES

Martel, E. (2001). From mensch to macho: The social construction of Jewish masculinity. *Men and Masculinities, 3*(4), 347–369.

Martín Alcoff, L. (2003). Latino/as, Asian Americans, and the Black-White binary. *The Journal of Ethics, 7*(1), 5–27.

Martinez, E. (1994). *Seeing more than Black & White: Latinos, racism, and the cultural divides.* http://www.indigenouspeople.net/blackwht.htm

Martins, N., & Harrison, K. (2012). Racial and gender differences in the relationship between children's television use and self-esteem: A longitudinal panel study. *Communication Research, 39*(3), 338–357.

Mason, D., & Ide, B. (2014). Adapting qualitative research strategies to technology savvy adolescents. *Nurse Researcher, 21*(5), 40–45.

Mastro, D. E., Behm-Morawitz, E., & Kopacz, M. A. (2008). Exposure to television portrayals of Latinos: The implications of aversive racism and social identity theory. *Human Communication Research, 34*(1), 1–27.

Mastro, D. E., Lapinski, M. K., Kopacz, M. A., & Behm-Morawitz, E. (2009). The influence of exposure to depictions of race and crime in TV news on viewer's social judgments. *Journal of Broadcasting & Electronic Media, 53*(4), 615–635.

Matias, C. E. (2016). *Feeling White: Whiteness, emotionality, and education.* Sense Publishers.

Maza, C. (2018, May 14). Dozens killed by Israel while protesting U.S. Jerusalem embassy move on Gaza's bloodiest day since 2014 war. *Newsweek.* http://www.newsweek.com/dozens-shot-dead-protesting-trumps-jerusalem-embassy-move-gazas-bloodiest-day-924461

McClaskey, R. (2008). A guide to discourse analysis. *Nurse Researcher, 16*(1), 24–44.

McGregor, S. L. T. (2003). Critical discourse analysis: A primer. *Kappa Omicron Nu, 15*(1), 1–11.

McIntosh, P. (1989). *White privilege: Unpacking the invisible backpack.* http://www.interpretereducation.org/wp-content/uploads/2016/03/white-privilege-by-Peggy-McIntosh.compressed.pdf

McIntosh, H. (2014). Representations of female scientists in The Big Bang Theory. *Journal of Popular Film & Television, 42*(4), 195–204.

McLaren, P. (1995). White terror and oppositional agency: Towards a critical multiculturism. In C. L. Sleeter & P. L. McLaren (Eds.), *Multicultural education, critical pedagogy, and the politics of difference* (pp. 33–70). State University of New York Press.

McLaren, P. (2001). Che Guevara, Paulo Freire, and the politics of hope: Reclaiming critical pedagogy. *Cultural Studies <-> Critical Methodologies, 1*(1), 108–131.

McLaren, P. (2005). *Capitalists and conquerors: A critical pedagogy against empire.* Rowman & Littlefield Publishers, Inc.

Meer, N. (2013). Racialization and religion: Race, culture and difference in the study of antisemitism and Islamophobia. *Ethnic and Racial Studies, 36*(3), 385–398.

Meer, N., & Modood, T. (2012). For "Jewish" read "Muslim"? Islamophobia as a form of racialisation of ethno-religious groups in Britain today. *Islamophobia Studies Journal, 1*(1), 35–53.

Meriwether, E. (Executive Producer). (2011–2018). *New girl* [TV series]. Fox.

Merriam, S. B. (1991). *Case study in education: A qualitative approach.* Jossey-Bass.

Merriam, S. B. (2009). *Qualitative research: A guide to design and implementation.* Jossey-Bass.

Morris, M. D., & Rubin, G. E. (1993). The turbulent friendship: Black-Jewish relations in the 1990s. *The Annals of the American Academy of Political and Social Science, 530,* 42–60.

REFERENCES

Moulin, D. (2016). Reported schooling experiences of adolescent Jews attending non-Jewish secondary schools in England. *Race, Ethnicity and Education, 19*(4), 683–705.

Muller, J. Z. (2010). *Capitalism and the Jews*. Princeton University Press.

Nakhaie, R., & Nakhaie, F. S. (2020, July 5). Black lives matter movement finds new urgency and allies because of COVID-19. *The Conversation*. https://theconversation.com/black-lives-matter-movement-finds-new-urgency-and-allies-because-of-covid-19-141500

Nicholson, C. (2016). The role of historical representations in Israeli–Palestinian relations: Narratives from abroad. *Peace and Conflict: Journal of Peace Psychology, 22*(1), 5–11.

Nieto, S., & Bode, P. (2011). *Affirming diversity: The sociopolitical context of multicultural education* (6th ed.). Pearson Education, Inc.

Noack, R. (2018, April 11). 'It is like we have regressed 100 years': Report warns of resurgent global anti-Semitism. *The Washington Post*. https://www.washingtonpost.com/news/worldviews/wp/2018/04/11/resurgent-traditional-antisemitism-behind-corrosion-of-jewish-life-report-warns/?utm_term=.6e4efd989a45

Norwood, S. H. (2009). 'American Jewish muscle': Forging a new masculinity in the streets and in the ring, 1890–1940. *Modern Judaism, 29*(2), 167–193.

Nye, M. (2018). Race and religion: Postcolonial formations of power and whiteness. *Method and Theory in the Study of Religion*. doi:10.1163/15700682-12341444

Orelus, P. W. (2015). Introduction: Critical pedagogy at the race and gender crossroads. In P. W. Orelus & R. Brock (Eds.), *Interrogating critical pedagogy: The voices of educators of color in the movement* (pp. 1–16). Routledge.

Özturgut, O. (2011). Understanding multicultural education. *Current Issues in Education, 14*(2), 1–10.

Pallade, Y. (2009). "New" anti-Semitism in contemporary German academia. *Jewish Political Studies Review, 21*(1/2), 33–62.

Perea, J. (1997). The Black/White binary paradigm of race: The normal science of American racial thought. *California Law Review, 85*(5), 127–172.

Perry, H. L., & White, R. B. (1996). The post-Civil Rights transformation of the relationship between Blacks and Jews in the United States. *Phylon, 47*(1), 51–60.

Pew Research Center: Religion & Public Life. (2013, October 1). *A portrait of Jewish Americans*. http://www.pewforum.org/2013/10/01/chapter-2-intermarriage-and-other-demographics/

Pew Research Center. (2015, April 2). *The future of world religions: Population growth projections, 2010–2050 – Jews*. http://www.pewforum.org/2015/04/02/jews/

Pfefferman, N. (2009, October). A private eye's adventures are author's dream. *Jewish Journal*, 28. http://www.jewishjournal.com/television/article/a_private_eyes_adventures_are_jonathan_ames_dream_bored_to_death_20091028/

Phillips, G. (2018, February 27). Antisemitism: How the origins of history's oldest hatred still hold sway today. *The Conversation*. https://theconversation.com/antisemitism-how-the-origins-of-historys-oldest-hatred-still-hold-sway-today-87878

Phillips, K. (2017, April 24). The 'hotbed of anti-Semitism' isn't a foreign country. It's U.S. college campuses, a new report says. *The Washington Post*. https://www.washingtonpost.com/news/acts-of-faith/wp/2017/04/24/the-hotbed-of-anti-semitism-isnt-a-foreign-country-but-u-s-college-campuses-report-says/?utm_term=.fb1995e4acc2

Potok, C. (2003). *My name is Asher Lev*. Anchor.

Punyanunt-Carter, N. M. (2008). The perceived realism of African American portrayals on television. *The Howard Journal of Communications, 19*, 241–257.

Pyke, K. D. (2010). What is internalized racial oppression and why don't we study it? Acknowledging racism's hidden injuries. *Sociological Perspectives, 53*(4), 551–572.

REFERENCES

Rapfogel, W. E. (2013, July 10). The ignored Jewish poor: Study finds half a million American Jews living in poverty. *The Jewish Daily Forward.* http://forward.com/articles/179934/the-ignored-jewish-poor/?p=all

Ravits, M. A. (2000). The Jewish mother: Comedy and controversy in American popular culture. *MELUS, 25*(1), 3–31.

Rebhun, U. (2014). Correlates of experiences and perceptions of anti-Semitism among Jews in the United States. *Social Science Research, 47*, 44–60.

Regan, L. B., & Romirowsky, A. (2020, September 11). College administrators must address anti-Semitism on their campuses. *Newsweek.* https://www.newsweek.com/college-administrators-must-address-anti-semitism-their-campuses-opinion-1530834

Reich, W. (2020, January 27). Seventy-five years after Auschwitz, anti-Semitism is on the rise. *The Atlantic.* https://www.theatlantic.com/ideas/archive/2020/01/seventy-five-years-after-auschwitz-anti-semitism-is-on-the-rise/605452/

Reid-Pharr, R. F. (1996). Speaking through anti-Semitism: The Nation of Islam and the poetics of Black (counter) modernity. *Social Text, 14*(4), 133–147.

Rifkin, M. (2017). Indigeneity, apartheid, Palestine: On the transit of political metaphors. *Cultural Critique, 95*, 25–70.

Rios, F., Trent, A., & Castañeda, L. V. (2003). Social perspective taking: Advancing empathy and advocating justice. *Equity & Excellence in Education, 36*(1), 5–14.

Rishon, S. (2015, November 6). Surveying Jews of color. *Tablet Magazine.* http://www.tabletmag.com/scroll/194735/surveying-jews-of-color

Rishon, S. (2016, August 10). Dear Jews, Black lives can't only matter when you're criticizing the movement. *Tablet.* https://www.tabletmag.com/sections/news/articles/dear-jews-black-lives-cant-only-matter-when-youre-criticizing-the-movement

Rising, D. (2019, November 21). Survey: About 1 in 4 Europeans hold anti-Semitic beliefs. *The Associated Press.* https://apnews.com/f18c9fa70b794974b214b6e9f1552cfd

Roach, M. (2019, May 2). Surge in anti-Semitic attacks has caused a 'sense of emergency' among Jews worldwide, new report says. *Time.* https://time.com/5580312/kantor-center-anti-semitism-report/

Roberts, R. (2017, August 12). Donald Trump accused of inflaming racial tensions amid violent clashes in Charlottesville, Virginia. *The Independent.* https://www.independent.co.uk/news/world/americas/donald-trump-accused-inflaming-racial-tensions-violent-clashes-in-charlottesville-virginia-white-a7890351.html

Robinson, M. (2019, May 27). German Jews warned not to wear kippahs in public following spike in anti-Semitism. *CNN.* https://www.cnn.com/2019/05/26/europe/germany-antisemitism-kippah-intl-scli-ger/index.html

Rockler, N. R. (2006). *Friends,* Judaism, and the holiday armadillo: Mapping a rhetoric of postidentity politics." *Communication Theory, 16*, 453–473.

Rodan-Benzaquen, S. (2020, March 2). Europe's lessons for the struggle against anti-Semitism. *The Atlantic.* https://www.theatlantic.com/ideas/archive/2020/03/what-europe-can-teach-america-about-fighting-anti-semitism/607162/

Rollock, N., & Gillborn, D. (2011). Critical Race Theory (CRT). *British Educational Research Association* [Online resource]. http://www.bera.ac.uk/files/2011/10/Critical-Race-Theory.pdf

Rosenberg, Y. (2017, August 14). 'Jews will not replace us': Why White supremacists go after Jews. *The Washington Post.* https://www.washingtonpost.com/news/acts-of-faith/wp/2017/08/14/jews-will-not-replace-us-why-white-supremacists-go-after-jews/?utm_term=.5554f4684a25

REFERENCES

Rosenblatt, G. (2020, March 15). Is it still safe to be a Jew in America? *The Atlantic*. https://www.theatlantic.com/ideas/archive/2020/03/anti-semitism-new-normal-america/608017/

Rosenblum, A. (2007). *The past didn't go anywhere: Making resistance to Antisemitism part of all of our movements*. http://www.buildingequality.us/prejudice/antisemitism/rosenblum/

Rosenwasser, P. (2002). Exploring internalized oppression and healing strategies. *New Directions for Adult and Continuing Education, 94*, 53–61.

Rossman-Benjamin, T. (2018, August 17). Anti-Zionist attacks at universities have increased – yet schools aren't doing anything. *The Hill*. https://thehill.com/opinion/civil-rights/402337-anti-zionist-attacks-on-campus-have-increased-yet-schools-arent-doing

Rubin, D. (2004). Between prominence and obscurity. In H. Bak (Ed.), *Uneasy alliance: Twentieth-century American literature, culture and biography* (pp. 255–268). Rodopi Press.

Rubin, D. I. (2013). Still wandering: The exclusion of Jews from issues of social justice and multicultural thought. *Multicultural Perspectives, 15*(4), 213–219.

Rubin, D. I. (2017). Whiter shade of pale: Making the case for Jewish presence in the multicultural classroom. *International Journal of Multicultural Education, 19*(2), 131–145.

Rubin, D. I. (2018a). From the beginning: Creating a diversity and multicultural education course at Jacksonville State University. *Education and Urban Society, 50*(8), 727–746. https://doi.org/10.1177/0013124517713612

Rubin, D. I. (2018b). The muddy waters of multicultural acceptance: A qualitative case study on Antisemitism and the Israeli/Palestinian conflict. *Journal of Ethnic and Cultural Studies, 5*(1), 1–15.

Rubin, D. I. (2019). Navigating the "space between" the Black/White binary: A call for Jewish multicultural inclusion. *Culture and Religion: An Interdisciplinary Journal, 20*(2), 192–206. https://doi.org/10.1080/14755610.2019.1624267

Rubin, D. I. (2021). The stereotypical portrayal of Jewish masculinity on *The Big Bang Theory*. *The Journal of Popular Culture, 54*(2).

Ruggieri, D. G., & Leebron, E. J. (2010). Situation comedies imitate life: Jewish and Italian-American women on prime time. *The Journal of Popular Culture, 43*(6), 1266–1281.

Salem, W. (2014). The role of the Arab peace initiative in light of the latest Israeli-Palestinian war. *Palestine-Israel Journal of Politics, Economics & Culture, 19/20*(4/1), 161–163.

Scham, P. (2015). Perceptions of anti-Semitism in the Israeli-Palestinian conflict. *Palestine-Israel Journal of Politics, Economics & Culture, 20/21*(4/1), 114–120.

Scheitle, C. P., & Ecklund, E. H. (2018). Perceptions of religious discrimination among U.S. scientists. *Journal for the Scientific Study of Religion, 57*(1), 139–155.

Sherwood, H. (2019, July 31). Antisemitic incidents in Britain up 10% on last year, finds charity. *The Guardian*. https://www.theguardian.com/news/2019/aug/01/antisemitic-incidents-in-britain-up-10-on-last-year-finds-charity

Schlosser, L. Z. (2003). Christian privilege: Breaking a sacred taboo. *Journal of Multicultural Counseling and Development, 31*(1), 44–51.

Schlosser, L. Z. (2006). Affirmative psychotherapy for American Jews. *Psychotherapy: Theory, Research, Practice, Training, 43*(4), 424–435.

Schlosser, L. Z., Ali, S. R., Ackerman, S. R., & Dewey, J. J. H. (2009). Religion, ethnicity, culture, way of life: Jews, Muslims, and multicultural counseling. *Counseling and Values, 54*(1), 48–64.

REFERENCES

Schlosser, L. Z., & Rosen, D. C. (2008). American Jews. In F. T. L. Leong (Ed.), *Encyclopedia of counseling: Changes and challenges for counseling in the 21st century* (4th ed., pp. 977–983). Sage Publications, Inc.

Schlosser, L. Z., Talleyrand, R. M., Lyons, H. Z., & Baker, L. M. (2007). Racism, antisemitism, and the schism between Blacks and Jews in the United States: A pilot intergroup encounter program. *Journal of Multicultural Counseling & Development, 35*(2), 116–128.

Schrank, B. (2007). "Cutting off your nose to spite your race": Jewish stereotypes, media images, cultural hybridity. *Shofar: An Interdisciplinary Journal of Jewish Studies, 25*(4), 18–42.

Schwartz, F. (2020, April 20). Coronavirus sparks rise in anti-Semitic sentiment, researchers say. *The Wall Street Journal.* https://www.wsj.com/articles/coronavirus-sparks-rise-in-anti-semitic-incidents-researchers-say-11587405792

Segal, D. A. (1999). Can you tell a Jew when you see one? Or thoughts on meeting Barbra/Barbie at the museum. *Judaism, 48*(2), 234–241.

Seifert, K. (2020, July 10). DeSean Jackson's anti-Semitic posts are a critical teaching moment – for everyone. *ESPN.* https://www.espn.com/nfl/story/_/id/29434436/desean-jackson-anti-semitic-posts-critical-teaching-moment-everyone

Sensoy, Ö., & DiAngelo, R. (2012). *Is everyone really equal? An introduction to key concepts in social justice education.* Teachers College Press.

Sensoy, Ö., & DiAngelo, R. (2014). Respect differences? Challenging the common guidelines in social justice education. *Democracy & Education, 22*(2), 1–10.

Shapiro, E. S. (1994, August). Blacks and Jews entangled. *First Things.* https://www.firstthings.com/article/1994/08/blacks-and-jews-entangled

Sherwood, H. (2020, February 5). Antisemitic incidents hit new high in 2019, according to study. *The Guardian.* https://www.theguardian.com/news/2020/feb/06/antisemitic-incidents-hit-new-high-in-2019-according-to-study

Sheskin, I. M., & Dashefsky, A. (2018). United States Jewish population, 2018. In A. Dashefsky & I. M. Sheskin (Eds.), *American Jewish year book 2018* (pp. 251–347). Springer.

Sheskin, I. M., & Felson, E. (2016). Is the boycott, divestment, and sanctions movement tainted by anti-Semitism? *Geographical Review, 106*(2), 270–275.

Shudak, N. J. (2014). The re-emergence of critical pedagogy: A three-dimensional framework for teacher education in the age of teacher effectiveness. *Creative Education, 5*, 989–999.

Sigelman, L. (1995). Blacks, Whites, and anti-Semitism. *The Sociological Quarterly, 36*(4), 649–656.

Silva, C. (2009). Racial restrictive covenants history: Enforcing neighborhood segregation in Seattle. *The Seattle Civil Rights & Labor History Project.* https://depts.washington.edu/civilr/covenants_report.htm

Singer, J. M. (2008). A hidden minority amidst White privilege. *Multicultural Perspectives, 10*(1), 47–51.

Sleeter, C. E. (2017). Critical race theory and the whiteness of teacher education. *Urban Education, 52*(2), 155–169.

Sleeter, C. E., & McLaren, P. L. (Eds.). (1995). *Multicultural education, critical pedagogy, and the politics of difference.* State University of New York Press.

Solomin, R. M. (2019). Who are Ashkenazi Jews? *My Jewish Learning.* https://www.myjewishlearning.com/article/who-are-ashkenazi-jews/

Solórzano, D. G., & Bernal, D. D. (2001). Examining transformational resistance through a critical race and LatCrit theory framework: Chicana and Chicano students in the urban context. *Urban Education, 36*(3), 308–342.

REFERENCES

Solórzano, D. G., & Yosso, T. J. (2001). Critical race and LatCrit theory and method: Counter-storytelling. *Qualitative Studies in Education, 14*(4), 471–495.

Solórzano, D. G., & Yosso, T. J. (2002). Critical race methodology: Counterstorytelling as an analytical framework for education research. *Qualitative Inquiry, 8*(1), 23–44.

Spalding, J. D. (2000). "Big, not so bad, Bill Goldberg." *Beliefnet*. www.beliefnet.com/entertainment/2001/11/big-not-so-bad-bill-goldberg.aspx

Spring, J. (2010). *Deculturalization and the struggle for equality: A brief history of the education of dominated cultures in the United States*. McGraw-Hill.

Stapinski, H. (2017, June 2). When America barred Italians. *The New York Times*. https://www.nytimes.com/2017/06/02/opinion/illegal-immigration-italian-americans.html

Stephens, B. (2020, October 26). Anti-Semitism and what feeds it. *The New York Times*. https://www.nytimes.com/2020/10/26/opinion/antisemitism-tree-of-life-shooting.html

Tanenbaum Center for Interreligious Understanding. (2013). *What American workers really think about religion: Tanenbaum's 2013 survey of American workers and religion*. https://www.tanenbaum.org/2013survey

Tausch, A. (2014). The new global antisemitism: Implications from the recent ADL-100 data. *Middle East Review of International Affairs, 18*(3), 46–72.

Thiessen, M. A. (2019, August 13). The rise of anti-Semitism on the left. *The Washington Post*. https://www.washingtonpost.com/opinions/2019/08/13/rise-anti-semitism-left/

Timm, J. C. (2015, March 18). *Jewish fraternity vandalized with swastikas*. http://www.msnbc.com/msnbc/vanderbilt-university-jewish-fraternity-vandalized-swastikas

Tobin, G. A. (1988). *Jewish perceptions of Antisemitism*. Plenum Press.

Tukachinsky, R., Mastro, D., & Yarchi, M. (2015). Documenting portrayals of race/ethnicity on primetime television over a 20-year span and their association with national-level racial/ethnic attitudes. *Journal of Social Issues, 71*(1), 17–38.

Uliss, J. (2015, October 19). "Big Bang" writer talks about show's Jewish bent – On and off the set. *The Jewish Week*. www.thejewishweek.com/news/briefs/big-bang-writer-talks-about-shows-jewish-bent-and-set

Valdivia, A. N. (2010). *Latina/os in the media*. Polity Press.

Van Dijk, T. A. (1993). Principles of critical discourse analysis. *Discourse & Society, 4*(2), 249–283.

Ward, M., & Levin, D. (2019). Anti-Semitism or free speech? College students cheer and fear Trump order. *The New York Times*. https://www.nytimes.com/2019/12/15/us/trump-anti-semitism-order-college-students.html

Walt, V. (2019, June 20). Europe's Jews are resisting a rising tide of anti-Semitism. *Time*. https://time.com/longform/anti-semitism-in-europe/

Wax-Thibodeaux, E. (2020, June 19). Young Hasidic Jews protest in support of Black neighbors, challenging history of racial tensions. *The Washington Post*. https://www.washingtonpost.com/national/young-hasidic-jews-challenge-history-of-community-tensions-with-protest-in-support-of-black-neighbors/2020/06/19/e16aea56-abdf-11ea-a9d9-a81c1a491c52_story.html

Webb, C. (1998). Montgomery Jews and civil rights, 1954–1960. *Journal of American Studies, 32*(3), 463–481.

Weber, L. E. (1991). "Gentiles preferred:" Minneapolis Jews and employment. 1920–1950. *Minnesota History*, 167–182.

Weinbaum, B. (1998). How the job market, antisemitism and affirmative action intersect: A glimpse in one life. *NWSA Journal, 10*(3), 183–191.

Weinstein, L., & Jackson, C. (2010). College student antisemitism and anti-Israeli sentiment. *College Student Journal, 44*(2), 565–567.

REFERENCES

Wills, A. (2009, July 28). Catching up with Wolowitz. *Jewish Journal*. https://jewishjournal.com/culture/summer_savings/71543/

Wilner, M. (2017, November 8). ADL: Data suggests spike in antisemitism across US. *The Jerusalem Post*. http://www.jpost.com/Diaspora/ADL-Data-suggest-spike-in-antisemitism-across-US-513648

Winston, C. N. (2016). Evaluating media's portrayal of an eccentric-genius: Dr. Sheldon Cooper. *Psychology of Popular Media Culture, 5*(3), 290–306.

Wolf, S. A., Coats, K., Encisco, P., & Jenkins, C. A. (2011). *Handbook of research on children's and young adult literature*. Routledge.

Wong, J. C. (2020, August 25). QAnon explained: The antisemitic conspiracy theory gaining traction around the world. *The Guardian*. https://www.theguardian.com/us-news/2020/aug/25/qanon-conspiracy-theory-explained-trump-what-is

Yadidi, N. (2017, June 29). DOJ report: Majority of hate crimes go unreported. *CNN*. https://www.cnn.com/2017/06/29/politics/doj-hate-crime-report/index.html

Yin, R. K. (2008). *Case study research: Design and methods* (4th ed.). Sage.

Yu, T. (2006). Challenging the politics of the "model minority" stereotype: A case for educational equality. *Equity & Excellence in Education, 39*(4), 325–33.

ABOUT THE AUTHOR

Daniel Ian Rubin, PhD, is an Adjunct Professor with the University of Redlands' School of Education and a sixth-grade English teacher at an International Baccalaureate middle school. His research interests include antisemitism, issues of social justice, multiculturalism, and diversity in both education and society, and critical and dialectical thinking.

Printed in the United States
by Baker & Taylor Publisher Services